West Virginia
Off the Beaten Path®

Help Us Keep This Guide Up to Date

Every effort has been made by the author and editors to make this guide as accurate and useful as possible. However, many things can change after a guide is published—establishments close, phone numbers change, hiking trails are rerouted, facilities come under new management, etc.

We would love to hear from you concerning your experiences with this guide and how you feel it could be made better and be kept up to date. While we may not be able to respond to all comments and suggestions, we'll take them to heart and we'll also make certain to share them with the author. Please send your comments and suggestions to the following address:

The Globe Pequot Press
Reader Response/Editorial Department
P.O. Box 480
Guilford, CT 06437

Or you may e-mail us at:
editorial@globe-pequot.com

Thanks for your input, and happy travels!

OFF THE BEATEN PATH® SERIES

West Virginia

SECOND EDITION

by Stephen and
Stacy Soltis

Foreword by
Senator Jay Rockefeller

The
Globe
Pequot
press

Guilford, Connecticut

Maps created by Equator Graphics © The Globe Pequot Press
Illustrations by Carole Drong
Cover and text design by Laura Augustine
Cover photo: Images © PhotoDisc, Inc.
Illustrations on pages 92, 119, and 139 drawn from photos by Larry Belcher and David E. Fattaleh (p. 139), courtesy of West Virginia Division of Tourism

Illustration on page 115 drawn from photo by Arnout Hyde, Jr.

Off the Beaten Path is a registered trademark of The Globe Pequot Press

Library of Congress Cataloging-in-Publication Data is available

ISBN 0-7627-0220-6

Manufactured in the United States of America
Second Edition/Second Printing

To Annie and Christopher,
and to all the Soltises, Beasleys, Guthries, and Halls
who at one time or another have called the hills home

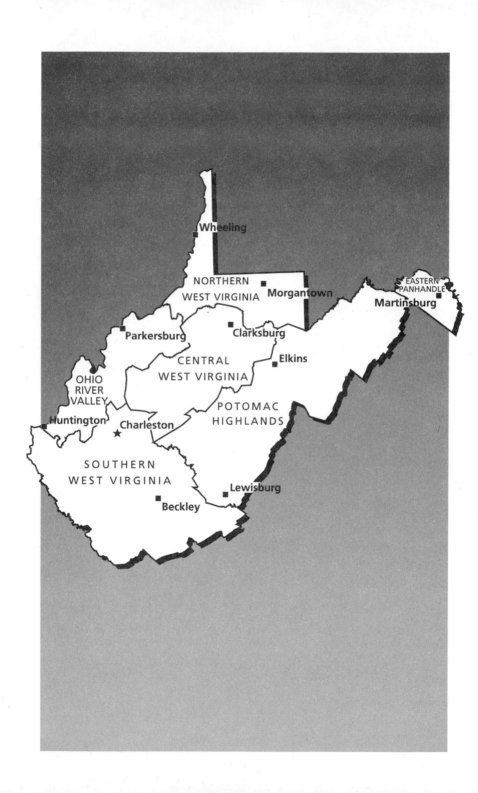

Contents

Foreword

There is a definite magic, a sense of wonder and adventure and tradition, about traveling the hidden backroads of America. It is a soothing tonic for the daily stresses and distractions of our high-energy lifestyles. We seek relief and escape along these quiet country roads, while always seeking out an adventure around the next bend.

My home state of West Virginia has history and heritage almost guaranteed to provide travelers with the ultimate off-the-beaten-path experience. Our rugged mountains, wild rivers, lush valleys, and warm, welcoming people are a prescription for "getting away from it all." With fewer than 1.8 million people living in towns and communities spread across more than 24,000 square miles, the Mountain State has seemingly limitless places to explore and enjoy.

In the pages that follow, you'll be introduced to scores of overlooked sights, sounds, tastes, and personalities that collectively offer a glimpse into the West Virginia experience. You'll travel from the hauntingly beautiful hollows of the southern coalfields to the aristocratic colonial pathways of the Eastern Panhandle. You'll experience the powerful natural magnificence of the New River Gorge and the simple, easy charms of quiet country inns. You'll hike the backcountry of the pristine Cranberry Wilderness and stroll beneath the gaslight lamps of Victorian Wheeling.

My guess is that you will come away as struck by West Virginia's wondrous beauty and relaxing pace of life as I did thirty years ago, when I first came to the state as a VISTA worker.

Naturally, West Virginia has changed a lot in that time. Modern interstate highways, a growing tourism industry, and new economic development attract millions of visitors to our state each year. While we may not be "undiscovered" any longer, there are more hidden natural and cultural gems woven into the Appalachians than you could get to in endless weekends.

I hope you will use *West Virginia: Off the Beaten Path* to lead you to some of the truly rare American riches found within these borders. It will be time well spent and a travel experience far removed from everyday life, restful and soothing and thick with history, hospitality, natural beauty, and adventure.

—Senator Jay Rockefeller

Acknowledgments

We could not have written *West Virginia: Off the Beaten Path™* without the hospitality, kindness, and insight of scores of friends and colleagues from throughout the Mountain State. We are especially indebted to the following people and organizations for their unparalleled guidance and assistance: Becky Kimmons of Kimmons and Associates in Charleston; Cara Rose of the Pocahontas County Tourism Commission; Cindy Harrington from the West Virginia Division of Tourism; Jack Deutsch, Washington correspondent for the *Charleston Daily Mail;* Leslie Haas of Fahlgren Martin; Jeanne Mozier of Travel Berkeley Springs; Pam Ritchie and Neal Roth of The Greenbrier; Martha and Sam Ashelman at Coolfont Resort, and all the good folks at the Cheat Mountain Club, Canaan Valley State Park, and Snowshoe Mountain Ski Resort. A special thanks goes to West Virginia historian and geographer Michael Gleason, who we're not sure has yet acccepted the fact that the mountaineers to the west have broken away from his beloved Old Dominion. We're also indebted to friends and family with whom we have shared unforgettable West Virginia traveling experiences over the years, including Matt and Deanna Soltis, Gordon and Betty Beasley, Roy and Kathy Dawson, Craig Leisher, Josh Rubin, John Marks, Bernard Burt, and Mariella and Gerardo Corrachano. A sincere thanks to all.

Introduction

Southerners and New Englanders in particular tend to wax romantically about the notion of a "sense of place." It's part of a mythical and somewhat inexplicable bond that constantly reminds them—and usually everyone around them—that yes, by gosh, they are "of good Yankee stock" or "Southern by the grace of God."

West Virginians, on the other hand, tend to take their "sense of place" for granted. They're a humble lot, never ones to try to inflict their "West Virginia-ness" on others. Uninformed outsiders may argue that they have to be this way; after all, there isn't much to romanticize about in this impenetrable land of "hillbillies, outlaws, and blood-letting coal miners."

West Virginians know all too well—as do most visitors to the state, or at least those who take the time to get off the interstate—that the degrading and tiresome stereotypes are bunk. West Virginians are among the friendliest and most helpful people to be found anywhere. They live in a state that has by far the lowest crime rate in the nation and the lowest cost of living. They live in a state that not only is beautiful but in many spots is simply drop-dead gorgeous.

In fact, West Virginia arguably has the most intense sense of place to be found anywhere in the United States. Wedged between the bustling urban megalopolis of the East and the industrial corridors of the Midwest, West Virginia, thanks to a rugged terrain, has remained sparsely populated and overwhelmingly pastoral in nature. Many first-time visitors remark that they know they're in West Virginia the minute they cross the state line. Sure, it's more rustic than its neighbors, but it's also greener, more relaxed, and infinitely more informal.

West Virginia is a rather small state, covering just over 24,000 square miles, roughly a quarter of the size of Colorado. It has been said, though, that if you took a gigantic rolling pin and flattened out the state's thousands of hills and mountains, the total surface area would be larger than that of Texas.

Because of its compact size, it's easy to think that there is a single cultural and social uniformity to West Virginia. That's just not true. There are distinctive divisions within the state: some geographical, some cultural, and some social.

For instance, the Eastern Panhandle, which extends to within only an hour's drive of metropolitan Washington, D.C.—and is actually closer to five other state capitals than it is to its own—is more aligned with the urban lifestyle of Northern Virginia and Maryland than it is with other parts of West Virginia.

On the other hand, folks residing in the industrialized Northern Panhandle consider themselves northerners, while those in Southern and Central West Virginia are decidedly southern in character. In the Ohio Valley, a case can be made that many of the people demonstrate Midwestern characteristics.

West Virginia has been described as "too Northern to be Southern, too Southern to be Northern, too Midwestern to be Eastern and too Eastern to be Midwestern." Maybe the best description is that West Virginia is simply West Virginia, or as locals like to say, "West By God Virginia."

If there is a common thread that links all West Virginians, it is a deep love and respect for the rich green hills, the foggy hollows, and the open space and sense of freedom that are such integral parts of this rural state. That freedom, in fact, is part of the state motto, *Montani Semper Liberi,* or "Mountaineers are always free."

This book's off-center journey through the Mountain State is designed to give a roadside sampler of the many often overlooked, unheralded, or simply unusual sites that abound here. In fact, just about everything in West Virginia is off the beaten path. Of course, that was more true fifteen years ago, before the completion of a couple of major interstates, but even with its newfound accessibility, West Virginia remains a truly undiscovered gem. It's a veritable gold mine for folks who love the mystery of the backroads, the out-of-the-way, the quaint, and the authentic in the truest sense of the words.

West Virginia: Off the Beaten Path™ begins in the Eastern Panhandle and progresses south and west through the Potomac Highlands, Southern West Virginia, and the Ohio Valley before turning north up through Central West Virginia and ending in Northern West Virginia.

Anyone who's ever been to West Virginia knows there is no such thing as a straight line between two points. Roads, towns, and farms either cling to mountainsides or wind along narrow river bottoms. Sometimes it's necessary to backtrack in order to see everything in a somewhat orderly fashion.

In this book you will tour the land where George Washington established his first farm, where a Nobel Prize–winning author drew much of her inspiration, where statesmen drafted resolutions to seek independence from slave-holding Virginia, where daredevil rafters and mountain climbers roam, and where families camp along pristine rivers and shop in creaky-floored country stores.

No matter what time of year you travel, there is something different and distinct to see, such as the breathtaking beauty of the state tree, the sugar maple, as it blazes red during the autumn months; the state animal, the black bear, and her cubs as they scamper across a gravel mountain road in the spring; or a fire-engine red cardinal perched on a blooming scarlet rhododendron in early summer.

The imagery here, of both the natural and man-made varieties, is extraordinary and plentiful. And it sticks with you long after you leave. It's enough to make you start believing that West Virginia isn't as much a state as it is a state of mind—one that's well worth exploring.

West Virginia at a Glance

- **West Virginia:** The Mountain State
- Admitted to the Union in 1863 after breaking from Virginia in 1861
- **Capital:** Charleston
- **Governor:** Cecil H. Underwood
- **Principal Cities:** Charleston, Huntington, Wheeling, Parkersburg
- **Population:** 1.8 million
- **Land Area:** 24,000 square miles
- **Climate:** average statewide daily minimum temperature: January—28 degrees F; average daily maximum temperature July—85 degrees F. Generally speaking winters can be severe in the Potomac Highlands and Allegheny Plateau, with annual snowfall ranging from 20 inches to over 200 inches in select areas. Eastern Panhandle, Southern West Virginia and Ohio Valley experience warm, humid summers, while the higher elevations tend to be relatively free of humidity and oppressive heat.
- **Major Newspapers:** *Charleston Daily Mail, The Charleston Gazette, Huntington Herald Dispatch, Wheeling Intelligencer, Wheeling News Register, Parkersburg News, Parkersburg Sentinel*
- **Public transportation** is limited in this rural state; Charleston, Wheeling and Huntington have municipal bus services. Charleston's

Chuck Yeager International Airport is the principal air gateway to the state.

- **Motto:** Mountaineers Are Always Free
- **State Song:** "The West Virginia Hills"
- **State Bird:** Cardinal
- **State Fish:** Brook trout
- **State Flower:** Rhododendron
- **State Tree:** Sugar Maple
- **Famous Natives:** Novelist Pearl S. Buck; Confederate General Thomas "Stonewall" Jackson; actor Don Knotts; pilot Chuck Yeager; diplomat Cyrus Vance.
- West Virginia Division of Tourism: 1–800–CALL–WVA; http://www.westvirginia.com

---

The prices and rates listed in this guidebook were confirmed at press time. We recommend, however, that you call establishments before traveling to obtain current information.

The Eastern Panhandle

The Eastern Panhandle, shaped somewhat like the perched head of a turtle, is West Virginia's easternmost region, and as such bears close association with neighboring Maryland and Virginia and even suburban Washington, D.C.

The three-county region is defined by the Potomac River to the north and the Shenandoah River, which flows in from Virginia along the eastern edge of Jefferson County. The far-western portion of the Panhandle (Morgan County) is mountainous and relatively isolated, while the central and eastern sections (Berkeley and Jefferson Counties) roll alongside the gentle terminus of the Blue Ridge Mountains and are pocketed with numerous small towns and a wealth of historical and cultural attractions.

Despite the fact that it's the state's most widely visited region, the Eastern Panhandle still offers an exhaustive array of hidden and/or unsung treasures. For first-time visitors to West Virginia, this is a good primer trip and a logical starting point if you're coming from the east.

The Shenandoah Valley

The fabled Shenandoah Valley, imprinted on the American psyche through song, stage, and screen, is more synonymous with neighboring Virginia than West Virginia. There's no doubt about it though, this historic and fertile valley rolls north into the Mountain State along with its namesake river, claiming all of Jefferson County and part of Berkeley County. Also known as the Valley of Virginia, the Shenandoah is one of several geographic entities that make up the Great Valley, a massive, erosion-carved trench stretching from south-central Pennsylvania to northeastern Tennessee. The Great Valley was a major southern migration route for Pennsylvania's Scottish-Irish and German settlers, brave and industrious pioneers who lived close to the land, tapping its rich soil for crops and dense hardwood forests for shelter, furniture, and farm implements.

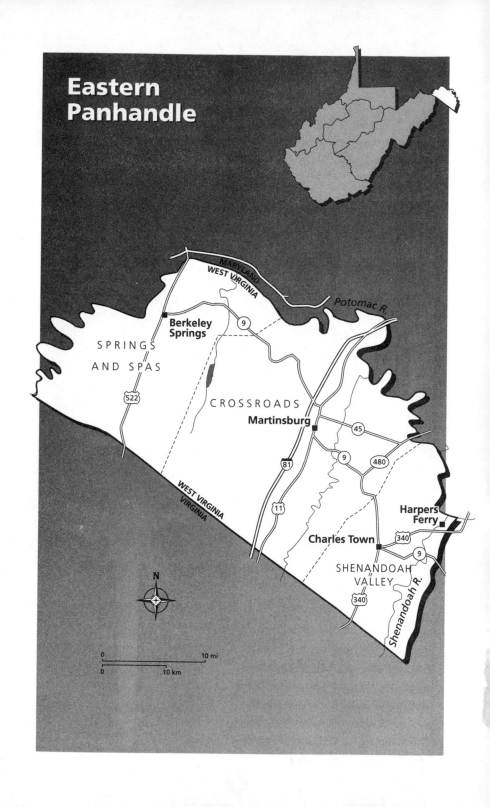

Eastern
Panhandle

MARYLAND
WEST VIRGINIA

Potomac R.

Berkeley
Springs

SPRINGS
AND SPAS

9

522

CROSSROADS
Martinsburg

45

81

9

480

11

WEST VIRGINIA
VIRGINIA

Harpers
Ferry

340

Charles Town

9

SHENANDOAH
VALLEY

340

Shenandoah R.

N

0   10 mi
0   10 km

THE EASTERN PANHANDLE

BEST ANNUAL EVENTS IN THE EASTERN PANHANDLE (ALL AREA CODES 304)

Winter Festival of the Waters, Berkeley Springs; January through March; 258-9147

Mountain Heritage Arts and Crafts Festivals, Charles Town; mid-June and late September; 725-2055

Contemporary American Theater Festival, Shepherdstown; through July; 876-3473

Apple Butter Festival, Berkeley Springs; second weekend in October; 258-3738

Mountain State Apple Harvest Festival, Martinsburg; mid-October; 263-2500

Christmas in Shepherdstown; late November through the first week of Decembeeer; 876-4553

West Virginia's swath of the Shenandoah (a Native American term meaning "Daughter of the Skies") is an important agricultural region and a mecca for artisans, writers, cottage-industry entrepreneurs, retirees, and weekend retreaters from nearby urban areas.

This is a land deeply proud of its colonial history and colorful folklife, evidenced by such huge fetes as the Mountain Heritage and Arts and Crafts Festival, held each spring and fall outside of Harpers Ferry. The laid-back valley is conducive to relaxation, whether it be a lazy day of floating on the Shenandoah River or unwinding at the Charles Town Races, where thoroughbred horses having been going neck and neck since 1786.

Above all this is a land of immense natural beauty. It was on the way back from a trip to Jefferson County that the late John Denver penned the words to "Country Roads," an international record-ing hit that begins with the classic line "Almost heaven, West Virginia." True sentiments, indeed.

At 247 feet above sea level, ***Harpers Ferry*** is the lowest point in the Mountain State. It's also West Virginia's easternmost city, wedged in the foothills of the Blue Ridge Mountains between Maryland and Virginia.

Harpers Ferry's 800 residents live less than an hour's drive from the suburbs of Washington, D.C., a blessing or a curse depending on whom you talk to. With urbanization slowly creeping westward, it seems fitting that this postcard village at the confluence of the Shen-andoah and Potomac Rivers is the headquarters of the ***Appalachian Trail Conference (ATC),*** a seventy-year-old, nonprofit conservation group dedicated to maintaining and preserving the natural character of the 2,144-mile-long Appalachian National Scenic Trail. The cele-brated foot trail, running from Springer Mountain, Georgia, to Mount Katahdin, Maine, was blazed by the ATC along the crests of the Appalachian Mountains in the 1930s, with help from several federal and state agencies and the Civilian Conservation Corps, the Depres-sion-era organization responsible for developing many of our national parks.

Today about two-thirds of the American population lives within 500 miles of the mountain wilderness sanctuary. Harpers Ferry is situated at nearly the halfway mark on the trail, and as such it is a natural gathering and refueling point for backpack-toting hikers. Much of the ATC's work is centered on ensuring that there is plenty of green and open buffer land for the tens of thousands of hikers who take to the trail each year, a mission that's backed by a major lobbying presence in the nation's capital. For anyone who's ever stepped foot on the Appalachian Trail, or even just thought about it, make sure to pay homage at its headquarters in the rustic cottagelike structure located on the corner of Washington and Jackson Streets. Inside you'll find interesting displays explaining the history and dynamics of the trail; a host of books, maps, posters, shirts, hats, and other hiking accessories; as well as information about volunteering and ATC programming. The headquarters is open Monday through Friday from 9:00 A.M. to 5:00 P.M. Call (304) 535–6331 for more information.

A short walk down the hill from ATC headquarters (follow the signs on Washington Street) is **Hilltop House,** an old, unpretentious mountain inn that straddles a rocky bluff overlooking the shallow and fast-mov-

R I V E R Spells Relief

"*Every man,*" said Winston Churchill, "*has his limitations.*" So too, I thought, did air-conditioning. August in Washington, D.C., is not for the faint of heart. You don't simply feel the heat and humidity, you wear it much like a hot wet blanket. It's on these days that not even air-conditioning can do the trick.

I had the urge to soak in cool natural water, not the warm bathtub stuff of swimming pools or the chlorinated spray of a backyard hose. I needed a cleansing West Virginia river gurgling over my shoulders and lapping over my head. That was the only tonic that could drive away the scorching misery.

By 3:00 P.M. on a Saturday, the weekend traffic rush from town had long subsided, and I figured I could reach Harpers Ferry in just over an hour, barring any idle state troopers. Seventy-two minutes later I'm lying in a two-foot limestone pool in the middle of the Shenandoah River. Trees along the hillsides are swaying to a late-afternoon breeze that spills down to the valley floor and rolls along with the river.

A half-dozen rafters float by, fully enjoying the final days of summer. A young high-school kid with a paddle waving in the air shouts, "Hey, mister, need a lift back to the shore?" I thank him but decline, explaining that I just wanted to lay there for the next three days.

"Cool," he says, and paddles away. A perceptive young man, indeed.

ing Potomac River. The place exudes charm, from the creaky wooden floors of the lobby to a partial fieldstone exterior dating back to 1888. Over the years Hilltop has provided respite for Alexander Graham Bell, Mark Twain, Pearl S. Buck, and Woodrow Wilson, among others. The river and mountain vistas afforded from the circular driveway alone are worth a night's stay, but take at least a couple of days if for no other reason than to enjoy the inn's hearty regional fare, which includes Virginia baked ham, pheasant, smoked trout, and Chesapeake Bay crab delicacies.

Into the Hills

*M*ost people who love the outdoors have at least dreamed of hiking the Appalachian Trail. This extraordinary wilderness pathway remains the signature mountain hike in America, and certainly one of the most famous in the world.

Although the trail's administrative offices are headquartered in Harpers Ferry, West Virginia is home to just a few miles of the AT. The state's rugged Allegheny Range was deemed too far west to extend the trail, which runs the entire span of the Blue Ridge Mountains through the southern and mid-Atlantic states. The Mountain State claims less than 50 miles of the trail, and most of that lies directly south of Harpers Ferry, paralleling the Shenandoah River and the dividing range with Virginia.

Hiking this section is rarely a solitary experience because it's within a ninety-minute drive from the Washington-Baltimore corridor. It is, however, an incredible entree to the beauty and magic of the trail.

It was here, along the downward stretch between State Route 9 and the confluence of the Shenandoah and Potomac Rivers, that we met up with

Deale Graves and his nine-year-old son, Ben. The Graves men of Falls Church, Virginia, were on their third day of a four-day hike, having started midweek back at Sky Meadows State Park near Paris, Virginia. Dad seemed a little more worn than Ben, who we learned had been hiking this trail since he was seven. Father and son were on to a great fall tradition, taking in time to see the fall colors and experience the final warms days of Indian summer

The Graves's annual hike was also about getting in touch with family roots. These low-lying hills were home to the first settlement of Graves's in Virginia. Family legend had it that the Graves homestead was once visited by members of John Brown's unsuccessful raiders. Supposedly, they came in peace or more likely to escape the law.

"People escaping to these hills is nothing new," said the elder Graves. "And I don't suppose folks will ever stop trying to find some peace up here."

Looking out over a rocky ledge—Virginia's glorious Hunt Country to the east and the last stand of the West Virginia's Shenandoah Valley to the west—I could not have agreed more.

The dining room menu, depending on the chef's temperament and the time of year, may also include dishes like curry chicken mousse on cucumber ovals, duck crepes with spicy plum sauce, and veal mousse pâté.

Hilltop's sixty-six rooms range from comfortable no-frills to an apartment-sized top-floor suite with spectacular picture-window views and a Jacuzzi. Make sure to budget time to browse through *The Old Stone Lodge,* a nineteenth-century landmark that doubles as the inn's gift shop, featuring colonial furniture and clocks and locally made jams, syrups, soaps, jewelry, pottery, and quilts. Room and dining rates are moderate. For reservations call (800) 338–8319.

From Hilltop you're maybe a five-minute walk to the center of the restored village, virtually all of which is contained in the *Harpers Ferry National Historical Park,* the single largest tourist draw in West Virginia. Although not exactly off the beaten path, a stroll through the National Park Service area is strongly advised for American history buffs, for it was here in 1859 that abolitionist John Brown raided the national armory and arsenal in an attempt to seize guns and munitions needed for his planned slave rebellion. Although the seizure was ultimately repelled by the U.S. Army under the command of a young Robert E. Lee, the action nevertheless was an important catalyst in the growing division over slavery—an issue that ultimately split open the nation with the advent of the Civil War.

A good place to begin touring the town (named after an early settler who operated a ferry service) is at the park service's information center on Shenandoah Street. Rangers answer questions and distribute orientation maps that lead to such sites as the Harpers Ferry Armory and Arsenal, which is at the corner of High and Shenandoah Streets and is located near the main-line tracks of the Baltimore & Ohio Railroad, and which served as the abolitionists' fort during the attempted seizure. Across the street the John Brown Museum chronicles Brown's raid, capture, trial, and hanging in neighboring Charles Town. Up yet another hill, this one overlooking the Shenandoah, stands *St. Peter's Catholic Church,* a gorgeous stone chapel built in 1830 and used continuously until its closing in 1994. A few steps away is the famous *Jefferson Rock,* a granite outcropping with a stunning, three-state view of the Blue Ridge Mountains and the merging rivers. Thomas Jefferson, who helped survey the area as a young man, sat upon the rock and wrote "this view is well worth a trip across the Atlantic." The National Park Service facilities are open daily year-round (except Christmas) from 8:00 A.M. to 5:00 P.M. and to 6:00 P.M. from Memorial Day to Labor Day.

THE EASTERN PANHANDLE

OTHER ATTRACTIONS WORTH SEEING
IN THE EASTERN PANHANDLE

A. T. Gift Company
Vineyard—Harpers Ferry

Homestead Farms Riding
Stable—Martinsburg

Rock Hill Creamery—
Martinsburg

Jefferson Growers'
Market—Charles Town

There are nominal parking and walk-in fees, payable at the Cavalier Heights Visitor Center on U.S. Highway 340. A free shuttle bus service transports visitors to the park area. For more information call (304) 535–6029.

Whether you're meandering through Harpers Ferry's peaceful hills or crowded streets and alleyways, it's impossible to escape the presence of the Shenandoah and Potomac Rivers. The Potomac, while on its 400-mile journey to the Chesapeake Bay from its source spring in Tucker County, West Virginia (see chapter on Potomac Highlands, pg. 43), takes on a wild-and-scenic demeanor as it flows through Harpers Ferry, churning up white water as it glides over limestone ridges and rocks. The same can be said of the Shenandoah, the northward flowing river that ends its 150-mile path from Rockingham County, Virginia, with a gentle white-water display that attracts anglers and rafters in droves. Harpers Ferry, you might remember, was the scene of devastating floods during the winter of 1996, when both the Shenandoah and Potomac crested at historically high levels. The flood damage, while extensive at the time, is now a mere memory. The Park Service Visitors Center, however, captures the catastrophe in great detail through a number of exhibits.

Fishing, tubing, canoeing, kayaking, and rafting trips can be organized on both rivers through *River & Trail Outfitters,* based just across the Potomac in Knoxville, Maryland. A best bet for an intermediate-level white-water experience is to canoe the Shenandoah Staircase, a 6-mile outing with several sets of Class I to III rapids (VI is the most advanced) and a few long stretches of flatwater for fishing. The float ends with a dramatic entrance into the Potomac Watergap at Harpers Ferry. River & Trail is accessible from the Maryland side of U.S. Highway 340. Turn left onto Valley Road at the blinking lights just beyond the Potomac River Bridge. Most float trips take place from spring to late fall. Outfitting fees are moderate; phone reservations should be made by credit card. Call (301) 695–5177 for more information.

West Virginia contains a treasure trove of off-beat museums, and one of the most obscure is *Harpers Ferry Toy Train Museum,* located 2 miles west of town on Bakerton Road just off U.S. Highway 340. Be prepared for a nostalgic trip back to childhood as you browse through the museum's large assortment of antique Lionel standard-gauge and O-gauge trains and accessories, most of them predating 1939. This was the personal collection of the late Robert E. Wallich, who in 1970 decided to share his sixty-year avocation with the public. The first Harpers Ferry Toy Train Museum was located in downtown Harpers Ferry and housed in a vintage Western Maryland Railroad baggage car. A few years later Wallich constructed an outdoor miniature railroad on his property in the outlying hills and eventually moved the museum to the same site. Wallich's son and grandson now run the museum and Joy Line Miniature Railroad, a train ride that's driven by a Cagney steam locomotive and appears to attract as many adults as kids. The museum is open April through November on Saturday, Sunday, and major holidays from 9:00 A.M. to 5:00 P.M. A small admission is charged. Special appointments for parties can be made any time of year. Call (304) 535–2291.

Leaving Harpers Ferry enroute to Charles Town on U.S. Highway 340, about a 5-mile trip, the landscape begins to open up, revealing rolling pastures and low, sloping mountains that form the outline of the Shenandoah Valley. Charles Town, the county seat of Jefferson County, sits in the heart of the West Virginia portion of the valley. The city was incorporated in 1787 and named in honor of George Washington's youngest brother, Charles, a major landowner in the Eastern Panhandle. Charles Washington donated eighty acres to the burgeoning village and was charged with laying out its original streets—George, Samuel, Lawrence, Mildred, and Charles—dutifully named after Washington family members. Not surprisingly, Charles Town's main thoroughfare is Washington Street. The city's current population of 3,200 is projected to increase as it acclimates to its newfound status as an exurb of metro Washington, D.C.

While in town buy a postcard and have it mailed from the *Charles Town Post Office,* 101 West Washington Street. This is where the Honorary William L. Wilson, Charles Town native and U.S. postmaster general, started the nation's first rural free delivery, or R.F.D., in 1896. On this site also stood the town jail where John Brown was imprisoned while awaiting his treason trial. The post office is open Monday through Friday from 8:30 A.M. to 5:00 P.M.; Saturday to 12:30 P.M. Call (304) 725–2421.

To dig more into the turbulent history of Brown and Charles Town, stop by the *Jefferson County Museum* on the corner of Washington and Samuel Streets. Among the hundreds of fascinating curios here are old black-and-white photographs depicting the county's agrarian roots, surveying maps, equipment used by George Washington, and the wagon used to transport John Brown to his execution. The museum is open 10:00 A.M. to 4:00 P.M., Monday through Saturday, April through November. Admission is free. Call (304) 725–8628 for more information.

THE EASTERN PANHANDLE

Eastern Panhandle Trivia

A sense of the macabre and gastronomic delight converge across the street at *The Iron Rail,* a restaurant that was formerly the home of a prominent nineteenth-century citizen, Andrew Hunter. Hunter House once sat on the farm where John Brown was hanged, and although martial law prevented the public from witnessing the execution, many residents viewed the scene from

The eighteen hole championship golf course located at Cacapon Resort State Park was created by the legendary golf-course designer Robert Trent Jones.

this huge Federal-style home on Washington Street. Of course the view's a little different today and undoubtedly so is the cuisine. Excellent beef and seafood dishes prevail, especially the fresh local trout and veal, and the ambience of dining in a 185-year-old building (and what looks like a transplant from New Orleans's Bourbon Street) adds to The Iron Rail's appeal. Prices are moderate. The Iron Rail is open for lunch from 11:00 A.M. to 3:00 P.M., Monday through Saturday, and dinner from 5:00 P.M. to 10:00 P.M., Wednesday through Saturday. Credit cards are accepted. For reservations call (304) 725–0052.

Two blocks west puts you in front of one of the most historic county courthouses in America. The original *Jefferson County Courthouse* was built here (corner of Washington and George Streets) in 1803, but heavy damages imposed by Union troops during the Civil War forced a massive restoration in 1871. With its red brick facade and stately white columns, this classic, Georgian, colonial structure was the site of two of the nation's three treason trials held before World War II. John Brown was sentenced to die here in 1859, and in 1922 several accused leaders of West Virginia's infamous coal mining wars in Mingo and Logan Counties were tried for treason. One man, Walter Allen, was convicted and sentenced to jail for ten years. Allen supposedly was part of a group of striking miners that took up arms in a series of bloody confrontations against federal and state troops called on to support the coal operators. The courthouse is open Monday through Thursday from 9:00 A.M. to 5:00 P.M. and to 7:00 P.M. on Friday. Admission is free. The phone number is (304) 725–9761.

Although the Eastern Panhandle is one of the most densely populated regions of West Virginia, it still retains a strong rural character underscored by thousands of acres of cattle farms, productive croplands, and apple and peach orchards. The pastoral legacy of the Virginia gentleman farmer lives on in places like *Hillbrook Inn on Bullskin Run,* a stunning English-style country manor house/hotel. Five miles southwest of Charles Town, off Summit Point Road (Route 13), Hillbrook sits amid seventeen acres of gardens, lawns, woods, and ponds. Bullskin

Run (in Virginia and West Virginia large brooks and streams are known as "runs") dissects the property, enhancing its quiet elegance.

Inside the inn guests might be greeted with the aroma of roasted pheasant from the kitchen or the sound of an oak-wood fire crackling in the tavern. A colorful mix of antiques and contemporary art fills the private rooms and walls, giving the place an aristocratic aura that beckons comparison to the manor homes of the Cottswalds. Hillbrook's six guest rooms all have private baths, sitting areas, and air-conditioning. Two rooms have queen-sized beds and fireplaces. Lodging rates are equally aristocratic, but they typically include a seven-course meal with wine and a country breakfast. If you plan to come just for lunch, dinner, or an English high tea (November through April), innkeeper Gretchen Carroll suggests making reservations well in advance. A contingency of affluent—and loyal—Washingtonians apparently has already discovered this hidden gem. Hillbrook is open year-round, except Christmas. Check-in is after 3:00 P.M. and checkout is noon. Call (304) 725–4223.

Hillbrook's land, and some 2,200 acres surrounding it, once belonged to the Bullskin, or **Rock Hall Tract,** the first real estate owned by George Washington. The young, and future president actually surveyed the region in 1750 and took part of his salary to purchase Rock Hall Tract from a Captain Rutherford, an early settler. A state historical marker, located in front of South Jefferson Elementary School on Summit Point Road, signals the site of Washington's first farm.

Changing eras a bit, there's another site a couple of miles west on Summit Point Road that is frequented by modern-day luminaries, including Paul Newman and Tom Cruise. If you guessed auto racing, you're right on track. Within earshot of the tiny hamlet of Summit Point, **Summit Point Raceway** unfolds a 2-mile-long course covering more than 375 acres. From early March to early December, the Sports Car Club of America (SCCA) sanctioned track hosts a variety of professional and amateur auto, motorcycle, and go-cart races. Each May the Jefferson 500 Vintage Sports Car Race rolls the clock back a bit with a pair of 500-kilometer races—one for cars built before 1965 and another for 1965–1980 models. More for fun than competition, a vintage race might begin with an airplane sweeping down and leading the cars off the starting grid. Newman and Cruise, meanwhile, pop in at least once a season to ride in the NASCAR circuit. You don't, however, have to be rich and famous to take to the curvy roads of Summit Point. The SCCA sponsors a series of race car driving schools for wannabe Andrettis, no pit crew required. If a seat in the grandstand is excitement enough, try revving up with bowl of the track's famous "100 m.p.h." chili and a cold beer. Admission to spectator events is moderate. Call (304) 725–8444 for event and driving-school information.

Exploring the backroads of West Virginia puts one in touch with a lot of water. Rivers, creeks, runs, ponds, and lakes are as ubiquitous here as are traffic lights in the big city. All that water might get you thinking about fish, something the Mountain State has in no short supply. If so, by all means take a 9-mile detour up to the **National Fisheries Center** in Leetown on the western fringe of the Shenandoah Valley. This 400-acre complex, sprawling across both sides of Leetown Road (Routc 1), is one of the U.S. Fish and Wildlife Center's premier fisheries development and health research facilities. Studies ranging from the effects of acid rain on brook trout to the impact of agricultural pollution runoff on striped bass are carried out by resident scientists, naturalists, and environmentalists. Exhibits and information materials of the work being

Left at the Bull

*I*t was a bright, crisp Sunday morning in early spring and it seemed all of Jefferson County was either in church or on its way to church. I was headed for a different kind of altar, the High Church of Eastern Panhandle motor sports—Summit Point Raceway. For first-time visitors, it's not exactly an easy place to find, even for Rand McNally-philes such as myself. After thirty minutes of wrong-way ramblings along the county's circuitous southern backroads, I broke down and decided to ask for directions.

The first person I came across was a nicely dressed elderly gentleman walking beside the gravel road. Obviously, he was on his way to an engagement far more pressing than mine. I pulled up beside him and sheepishly asked for the way to Summit Point Road. The handsome gentleman smiled and pointed straight ahead. "Take this road a fair piece and turn left at the bull."

What bull? Or did he say "boulevard"?

I'd already invested some quality time getting lost, so I decided not to second-guess him. Besides he was already late for church. I drove west down the farm road for about 2 miles before dead-ending into a hard-scrabble pasture. Sure enough, sitting dead-center in front of my car was probably the largest Black Angus bull I'd ever seen—2,500-pounds of beef, chewing on massive cud of dandelions and Bermuda grass. The bull had that look of total boredom, no doubt the result of watching dozens of similarly confused motorists every day.

To the left, beside the fenced pasture, a small dirt road rolled and rutted for a few hundred yards before reaching Summit Point Road. I wasn't sure if I had just trespassed on private land or not, and I didn't really care. The old man's directions were right-on, "Turn left at the bull."

BEST ATTRACTIONS IN EASTERN PANHANDLE (ALL AREA CODES 304)

Harpers Ferry National Historical Park,
Harpers Ferry; 535–6223

Cacapon Resort State Park,
Berkeley Springs; 258–1022

Coolfont Resort, Spa and Conference Center, Berkeley Springs; 258–4500

Blue Ridge Outlet Center,
Martinsburg; 263–7467

Charles Town Race Track,
Charles Town; 725–7001

John Brown Wax Museum,
Harpers Ferry; 535–6342

O'Hurley's General Store,
Shepherdstown; 876–6907

done here are available at the visitors center, located on the west side of the road. A separate aquarium building and an environmental education section are also open to the public, as are special tours and a series of outdoor nature trails. The center is open May to October, Monday through Friday, 8:00 A.M. to 4:00 P.M.; Saturday and Sunday, 10:00 A.M. to 5:00 P.M. For more information, including off-season hours and special events, call (304) 725–7061.

Before heading north on Route 1 to Shepherdstown, duck down to the nearby **Harewood** estate, located on Route 51 between Middleway and Charles Town. The Georgian mansion was built in 1770 by Samuel Washington, the next oldest brother of George Washington, and the first in the family to move to the Eastern Panhandle. Like all Washingtons, Samuel was active in public affairs, appointed to serve as both county lieutenant and justice of the peace. He died in 1781, and his unmarked grave lies in a family plot on the property. In 1794 Harewood hosted the wedding of James Madison and Dolley Payne Todd, whose sister, Lucy Payne Washington, was the mistress of the estate. The home has been continuously occupied and to this day is owned by a direct descendant. Unfortunately, Harewood is not open to the public, but its exterior and grounds can be viewed from the road.

Shepherdstown lies up near the northern tip of Jefferson County, perched beautifully—and sometimes precariously—on the banks of the Potomac River. (The entire northern Potomac Basin is susceptible to dramatic flooding, and for folks living along the river roads, heavy spring rains can turn their homes into islands.)

Laid out by Thomas Shepherd in 1734, Shepherdstown is the oldest burgh in West Virginia, and its painstakingly preserved eighteenth-century homes and shops have rightfully been deemed a registered district on the National Register of Historic Places.

History seeps out of every nook and cranny here. When General Washington called for more support for the defense of Boston in 1775, Shepherdstown paid heed. The famous Bee Line March of Southern volunteers to Massachusetts began at Morgan's Spring, now part of **Morgan's Grove Park,** 1 mile south of town on Route 480. Shepherdstown went on to supply more troops to the Revolutionary War than any city its size in the colonies. At one point Washington even considered that the humble town should become the nation's new capital city.

During the Civil War, Shepherdstown was a strategic river-crossing into Maryland. Immediately after 1862's tragic battle of Antietam (just 5 miles away), in which more than 22,000 Americans were casualties of a single day's fighting, Shepherdstown became one massive hospital. Perhaps because of its empathetic nature, the town was spared major damages during the war.

This is equally fortunate for modern-day residents and tourists, who are blessed with some of the most scenic surroundings in West Virginia. Over the years Shepherdstown's quiet appeal has lured scores of artisans, writers, merchants, musicians, and scholars—folks who've helped stamp a distinctive impression on the place. Today about 1,800 people call the town home. One friend commented that Shepherdstown has become "West Virginia's answer to Stockbridge [Massachusetts]," a mixture of Rockwellian idyll and bohemian funkiness.

The lifeblood of Shepherdstown has always been *Town Run.* The pristine, spring-fed brook runs through the town's alleyways, backyards, and parks, and is used as an auxiliary water supply. During the village's infancy, Town Run powered *Thomas Shepherd's gristmill* (midblock of Mill Street), the area's first industry. (Interestingly, the gristmill, now a private home, still contains its 40-foot-diameter, cast-iron waterwheel, the largest of its kind in the world.)

At *Town Run Deli,* corner of Princess and High Streets, the namesake brook flows directly through the restaurant on its way downhill to the river. The waterway is covered to keep out pollutants, but the deli is open to hearty appetites, many coming from the nearby campus of Shepherd College. For a delicious and inexpensive meal, you can't go wrong with a "Wolman," described in the menu as an "adaption of a Philly original." The generous, grilled chicken-breast sandwich is loaded with melted Muenster cheese, cole slaw, and Thousand Island dressing. It's certainly enough to make one forget about Philadelphia for a while. Top it off with a slice of creamy lemon meringue pie. Prices are inexpensive. The deli is open Monday through Friday, 7:00 A.M. to 8:00 P.M.; Saturday, 8:00 A.M. to 4:00 P.M.; and Sunday, 11:00 A.M. to 3:00 P.M. Phone (304) 876–3200.

Some twenty years before Robert Fulton's steamship, The Clermont, cruised up the Hudson River, Shepherdstown resident James Rumsey built and successfully demonstrated a working steamboat on the Potomac. A replica of that boat is located across the street from Town

Run Deli at the **Rumsey Steamboat Museum** (located in the backyard of the Entler Hotel). Inside the boathouse/museum you'll also find displays and sketches outlining Rumsey's fascinating life and inventions. In the 1780s George Washington appointed the budding engineer and inventor to manage the development of a navigation company on the Potomac. Washington hoped the company would be a key asset in opening up the West through an elaborate canal system. Rumsey, however, was enchanted with the notion of mastering the river's strong currents by way of a steam-driven piston that created a water-jet propulsion system. On December 3, 1787, Rumsey and a crew of eight Shepherdstown ladies boarded a small test boat appropriately named the *Rumseian Experiment* and chugged up the Potomac at a formidable three knots. With Washington's encouragement, Rumsey took the knowledge of his technological breakthrough and went to London to secure financial aid to build a larger and commercially viable ship. Ironically, Rumsey died on the eve of completing the new improved steamboat and the project was soon aborted. These and other tales await visitors to the museum.

If you're lucky enough to be in Shepherdstown in the summer, the Rumseian Society (the group that runs the museum), under the guidance of Captain Jay Hurley, takes the steamship replica out onto the river for live demonstrations. The museum, with its new colorful outdoor mural depicting the Shepherdstown riverbank as seen through Rumsey's eyes, is open from April through October, Saturday and Sunday, 10:00 A.M. to 5:00 P.M. Captain Hurley says individual and groups tours also can be arranged in advance any time of year. Call (304) 876–6907 for more information and demonstration schedules. No admission is charged. (Hurley, incidentally, is the proprietor of O'Hurley's General Store, a popular stop on most daytrip circuits through Shepherdstown.) While down near the water, be sure to visit the **James Rumsey Monument** at the end of Mill Street. The tall Ionic column supports a granite globe of the world, a reference to the international reach of Rumsey's invention.

At Princess and German Streets sits Shepherdstown's famous **Yellow Brick Bank Restaurant,** a continental eatery inhabiting a former— you guessed it—yellow-brick bank. During the Reagan years in Washington, the First Lady and lunch pal George Will dined here frequently, thus putting the place on the social circuit and well onto the beaten path. Nevertheless, if you decide to brave the swarm of trendy tourist diners, the lunchtime menu features an incredible sweet corn and jalapeño chowder and an equally blissful Monte Cristo sandwich. Prices are moderate. Lunch is served 11:00 A.M. to 4:00 P.M., Monday through

Saturday; a Sunday brunch runs from 11:00 A.M. to 5:00 P.M. Dinner is served nightly 5:00 P.M. to 11:00 P.M. Credit cards are accepted.

Before leaving town, you'll want to stroll through the bucolic grounds of **Shepherd College,** founded in 1872 as one of the state's first liberal arts institutions. It was in the building that is now the campus's old main, McMurran Hall, at the corner of Duke and German Streets, that thousands of wounded soldiers were treated in the aftermath of Antietam. The school is widely recognized for its progressive programs in the natural and social sciences and in the arts and humanities. For the past several years, the college has played host to the Contemporary American Theater Festival, a show-

James Rumsey Monument

case of new works by some of the country's most important playwrights. Performances are staged by the state's only Actors' Equity theater, a talent pool drawn from Shepherdstown and across the country. Past productions have included such ambitious and poignant works as Black by Joyce Carol Oates and Dream House by Darrah Cloud. "We want to help renew the American theater by providing a haven for artists to collaborate and take risks," says Ed Herendeen, the festival's producing director. The nearly month-long thespian festival is typically held in July and also includes staged readings, improvisational comedy, and concerts. For more information about the Contemporary American Theater Festival, call (800) 225–5982, or contact the college at (304) 876–2511.

Crossroads

rossroads is the name we've given to the region that sits in the heart of the Eastern Panhandle and contains the historic railroad town of Martinsburg and all of Berkeley County west of U.S. Highway 11, sometimes still referred to as the "Valley Pike." In the early eighteenth century, the region became home to the first settlers in what is now West Virginia and later evolved into a bustling center of wagon, coach, and rail travel to the West. The Valley Pike, now paralleled by Interstate 81, once served as the major north/south artery linking Pennsylvania's Cumberland Valley to the Valley of Virginia.

The legacy of the earliest settlers lives on in Berkeley County's more than 2,000 National Register historic sites, the highest concentration in the state. Crossroads's vast fruit orchards, cattle ranches, and truck farms, meanwhile, continue to find steady markets in the growing urban corridors of the East, and in recent years they have become the focus of open-space preservation efforts. The gigantic *Mountain State*

Thanks to Dan Sheetz

*M*y buddy Josh and I were driving on Apple Pie Road, northwest of Winchester, Virginia, when we crossed back into the Mountain State near Glengary in Berkeley County. The heat of summer was still lingering on this lazy September afternoon as were our appetites after a morning of fly-casting for small-mouth bass on the Cacapon River. We were now enroute to Back Creek to see if any trout were still holding up in that stream's cool spring-fed waters.

It didn't help that we were parched and hungry and had barely enough money left over for the necessary trout flies. Apple orchard country spread out before us, and the delicious "Berkeley Reds" were tempting from both sides of the road.

We hatched a plan to pick a few apples right then and there. Not a sign of civilization within sight, and we reasoned that no apple grower would miss a few among the millions of tree-ripe apples. Josh zigged left, I zagged right, and after less than a minute in the orchard thickets, we were back at the car with a dozen or so red beauties.

Of course, we didn't expect Dan Sheetz to pull up in front of us while we were planning our getaway. Mr. Sheetz, it turned out, had been growing apples on his 100 acres for more than twenty years. Fortunately for us, he had a kind, weathered look of a man who loved the outdoors and admired anyone who shared his passion.

"Looks like you boys been fishin'," said Sheetz with a slight smile.

"Yes, sir," I piped up from the driver's seat. "We're thinking about heading over to Back Creek and looking for trout."

Sheetz's smile broadened and he said, "Before you head over that way, better take some of these downed branches as well. You catch some of those trout, and you'll want to smoke them over applewood coals. There ain't a finer smoke than applewood."

We took Dan Sheetz's advice—along with his apples and branches. By nightfall we added a few more fish to our creel. The applewood smoke turned a delicious trout into a heavenly trout. Mr. Sheetz's apples weren't bad, either.

Apple Harvest Festival, held every fourth weekend in October in Martinsburg, salutes one of the region's most successful agribusinesses.

With a population of 14,000—and growing—Martinsburg has long been the Eastern Panhandle's principal city, an industrial, agricultural, and transportation center that's just beginning to tap its tourism attributes. Because of its strategic importance as the western gateway to the neighboring Shenandoah Valley, Martinsburg was heavily impacted by the Civil War, once serving as a command center for Confederate General Thomas "Stonewall" Jackson, a native West Virginian. Though badly bruised during the war, the city remarkably preserved many of its glorious eighteenth- and nineteenth-century buildings.

One such structure is *Tuscarora Church,* 2335 Tuscarora Pike, about 2 miles west of downtown. Built from native limestone in 1740 by Scottish-Irish Presbyterians, the country church was refurbished in 1803 and is still going strong with more than 140 parishioners, according to Pastor Bruce McClendon. Here's one bit of evidence that even the farthest eastern reaches of West Virginia were once the "Wild West": On the back walls of the church are the two original gun racks worshippers used to hang their pistols during services. The state's oldest Presbyterian church holds Sunday service at 11:00 A.M. Call (304) 263–4579.

Another Martinsburg historical gem is the *General Adam Stephen House,* 309 East John Street, a native limestone home built between 1774 and 1789 by the town's founder. Construction was prolonged by the Revolutionary War, in which General Stephen served as soldier and surgeon. Like most Virginia gentlemen, General Stephen was more intent on creating a home with a natural aesthetic than a grandiose design. This simple, four-room rectangular house is perched on a hill overlooking Tuscarora Creek.

Next to the home on the same property is the *Triple Brick Building,* built in 1874 by Phillip Showers, who at the time owned the Stephen House. The three-story building supposedly got its name because it contained three apartment units used by workers rebuilding Martinsburg's Civil War–torn railroad yards. It's now used as a local history museum, complete with quilts, period clothes, Civil War memorabilia, and musical instruments. Both the General Adam Stephen House and the Triple Brick Building are open 2:00 P.M. to 5:00 P.M., Saturday and Sunday, May through October. Special viewing appointments can be made by calling (304) 267–4434. No admission is charged.

Three blocks to the north (200 block of East Martin Street) and across the tracks of the Baltimore & Ohio Railroad stands the *Roundhouse,*

Nineteenth-century Bunker Hill Mill, located near Martinsburg, is the only mill in the state featuring dual water wheels.

one of the finest examples of nineteenth-century industrial railroad architecture. Unfortunately abandoned years ago, the unmistakably round building was the nerve center of passenger and freight activity along the B & O route connecting Martinsburg to Baltimore in 1842. Most of the rail yard was destroyed by Jackson's troops during the Civil War, but the Roundhouse was rebuilt in 1866 and eleven years later it was the scene of a major rail-worker strike.

Situated less than a mile away in the rolling hills east of the railroad tracks is the **Old Green Hill Cemetery** on Burke Road. It's patterned on the Parisian mold with an impressive display of stone-carved art. The expansive views of Martinsburg and its environs from atop the cemetery's hills are spectacular. Among those buried here are President Lincoln's bodyguard, Ward Hill Lamon; writer/artist David Hunter Strother (a.k.a. Porte Crayon) of *Harpers Weekly* fame; at least thirty unknown Confederate soldiers; and the parents of Belle Boyd. The grounds are open dawn to dusk.

Belle Boyd, you might remember, was a Confederate spy working in cahoots with Stonewall Jackson. She was arrested and imprisoned twice but both times released for lack of evidence. After the war the Martinsburg native married one of her Union captors, went on to become a stage actress in New York and London, and later lectured and wrote a book about her spying exploits. Boyd's father, Benjamin Reed Boyd, built a twenty-two-room Greek mansion in the center of the city, and in recent years the Berkeley County Historical Society has restored the **Belle Boyd House,** 126 East Race Street, turning a portion of it into a Civil War museum and historical archive. The house contains original family heirlooms, journal entries, and wartime artifacts. Upstairs is a historical archives section. Hours are 10:00 A.M. to 5:00 P.M., Saturday and Sunday, May through December 24.

As you wend your way back to Interstate 81, detour to 330 Winchester Avenue and stop in at **Wright's Stained Glass and Custom Art** store and studio. Proprietors Jody and Carl Wright craft original hand-cut, stained-glass pieces made from world-renowned West Virginia glass. Their studio/shop is located in a hundred-year-old smokehouse tucked behind their Victorian home on the corner of Winchester and Stephen Streets. The Wrights explain that their customized stained-glass pieces are really "colored glass"—that the color is throughout, not a surface treatment, so the pieces won't fade with time. The Wrights also produce handmade hardwood furniture, pottery, quilts, woven materials, and mirrors based on customer specifications. The shop and studio are open Monday and Wednesday through Friday, 10:00 A.M. to 5:00 P.M.; Tuesday and Thursday by appointment only.

The intimacy of Wright's studio is light-years removed from Martinsburg's famous **Blue Ridge Outlet Center,** just a block away. Each year more than a million bargain-frenzied shoppers take to the five-dozen outlet retailers that have set up shop in this labyrinth of former woolen mills. Deals can be had, but go expecting a thundering press of humanity along with the bargains.

From Martinsburg jump on the interstate or the slower but more scenic U.S. Highway 11 and head 8 miles south to Bunker Hill, a village known for its apple orchards and antiques shops. Three miles west of town, on Old Mill Road (Route 26), is the rustic cabin home of West Virginia's first white settler, Colonel Morgan Morgan, a Delaware native who moved his family to this lonely western outpost in the 1730s. **Morgan Cabin,** now a living history museum of the Berkeley County Historical Society, was made from local hardwoods and stone in 1734, much of which remains in the restored version that is listed on the National Register of Historic Places. Save for a twentieth-century farmhouse located across the road, little seems to have changed in the past 260 years in this rural corner of Berkeley County. Standing in front of the cabin, one can almost imagine a clandestine Indian meeting taking place beyond the hills a few hundred yards to the south. One of the most violent clashes at Morgan's Cabin took place during the Revolutionary War when one of Colonel Morgan's grandsons, an American soldier, was captured by Tories and executed in front of his family. The pioneering Morgans nevertheless went on to become one of the Eastern Panhandle's most prominent families. Neighboring Morgan County and Morgantown, in Northern West Virginia, were named after them. Morgan Cabin is open Sunday, May through August, 2:00 P.M. to 5:00 P.M. Special tours can be arranged year-round by calling (304) 229–8946.

Heading back into Bunker Hill, you'll pass **Christ Church** on the left. Built in 1740 and frequented by the Morgan family, it's believed to be West Virginia's first house of worship, predating Tuscarora Church by a few months. The brick Greek Revival church has been restored three times and is undergoing a fourth renovation after suffering severe fire damage. Behind the church is the cemetery where Colonel Morgan and his wife are buried. **Bunker Hill Antiques Associates,** a local landmark, is directly next door at the corner of U.S. Highway 11 and Old Mill Road. The nineteenth-century mill-turned-emporium houses more than 170 furniture, jewelry, glass, book, and art dealers. It's open daily 10:00 A.M. to 5:00 P.M.; on Friday it stays open until 9:00 P.M.

From Bunker Hill head back to the Interstate 81 on-ramp, but instead of getting on the freeway continue west along the surface road (Route 51) for about 5 miles. You'll roll through beautiful dairy farm country before arriving in tiny **Gerrardstown.** There was a time when this Grandma Moses–like village wasn't quite so tiny. According to the proprietors of **Prospect Hill,** Gerrardstown's gorgeous Georgian bed-and-breakfast, the town of 200 people once boasted a population of more than 9,000. In the early nineteenth century, it was a booming wagon train crossroads, that is until the railroad came to then-smaller Martinsburg. Gerrardstown's rural flavor can be sampled, albeit in high style, at Prospect Hill, built in 1789 and situated on a 225-acre farm and orchard. The grand, redbrick home is awash in Chinese and Indian art, Oriental rugs, and American antiques, including colonial pieces in the two large guest rooms. Rates are moderate and include a breakfast and tea. The inn is open year-round. For reservations call (304) 229–3346.

Scan a map of West Virginia and you're bound to find dozens of towns with provocative names—places like Burnt House, Toll Gate, Tornado, Hurricane, Mud, and Twilight. In Crossroads there is **Shanghai,** about 10 miles northwest of Gerrardstown. The name alone inspires an investigation. One colleague suggested that it might have been founded by homesick Chinese railroad workers. Don Wood, executive director of the Berkeley County Historical Society, however, says there were no such workers here but that the name might have come from a local furniture manufacturer supposedly called Shanghai. Another theory, says Wood, is that several citizens of the village were locked up in jail so they could not vote and thus were "Shanghaied." To get to Shanghai, take Route 51 west 2 miles to Route 45. Hang a left here and continue 3 miles to Glengary, where you'll take the first right onto a narrow county road that leads north about 5 miles to Shanghai. Don't expect a bustling metropolis; Shanghai's basically a couple of houses, a store, and small post office. The sense of being on the frontier is the main attraction, a feeling that increases as you head west over Sleepy Creek Ridge into Springs and Spas.

Springs and Spas

There's always been a certain mystique, a certain magical attraction, to the western edge of the Eastern Panhandle. Maybe it has to do with the legends left behind by the Tuscarora and Shawnee Indians who, along with other warring Appalachian tribes, regularly visited the region's "healing waters" in peace. Maybe it stems from the colonial tradition set by George Washington and Thomas Jefferson of "taking to the baths," the plentiful warm springs that cleansed, soothed, and revitalized the body.

Whatever it is, this land of springs and spas is evolving into one of the East's leading health resorts, art and antiques centers, and outdoor recreation areas. Its 231 square miles comprise all of Morgan County. The northern and western borders are formed by the winding Potomac River, and its rugged spine is shaped by the uplift of the Shenandoah Mountains. The scenic beauty of the landscape and the diversity of residents, from white-collar urban transplants to seventh-generation farmers, make for an unforgettable travel experience.

Berkeley Springs, the area's largest town, bills itself as "the country's first spa." It's a not a hollow claim. Shortly after George Washington's family and friends drew up a plat of 134 lots, named the streets, and incorporated the town of Bath, the community emerged a haven for seekers of respite from a young and troubled nation. President George and First Lady Martha were such regular visitors during the presidency that historians dubbed Berkeley Springs the first "summer White House."

The focal point of Bath (still its official name) has always been the warm mineral springs found in the center of town on Washington Street at what is now *Berkeley Springs State Park,* a seven-acre spring and bathhouse compound that is also the nation's oldest state park. The outdoor springs flow from the base of Warm Springs Ridge at a rate of 1,500 gallons a minute, surfacing at a constant 74 degrees. The park's Lord Fairfax public tap is a gathering point for locals and tourists who come to fill their jugs with the sweet-tasting mineral water. But the star attraction is the 1815 *Roman Bath House* and its private bathing chambers with water heated to a relaxing 102 degrees. The two-story bathhouse is the oldest public building in Morgan County. On the second floor is the *Museum of the Berkeley Springs,* which chronicles the development of the town and its springs through old photographs, sketches, exhibits, and water-bottling memorabilia. On the opposite side of the park is the Main Bath House, offering water, steam, and therapeutic massage treatments; showers; and an exercise room. The park's baths are open from 10:00 A.M. to 6:00 P.M. daily, except Christmas and New Year's Day. Water treatments are inexpensive and popular, so it's best to reserve a private bath at least two weeks in advance. The museum is open daily, except for Wednesday, from Memorial Day through mid-October. Hours are 9:00 A.M. to noon on Monday and

Tuesday; 2:00 P.M. to 5:00 P.M. on Thursday and Friday; 10:00 A.M. to 4:00 P.M. on Saturday; and noon to 4:00 P.M. on Sunday. The park's number is (304) 258–2711.

Next door to the springs, the stately *Country Inn,* 207 S. Washington Street, triples as a hotel, spa, and restaurant. The inn's signature white-

Soothing Waters

*B*erkeley Springs's Festival of the Waters is perhaps the premier mid-winter festival in the country. It's also a wonderful tribute to the birth of George Washington and his lasting impact on this picturesque spa town.

One of the more colorful events of the festival is the municipal tap water tasting competition in which communities across the country submit their drinking water for honors consideration. In 1993 I was privileged to be selected as one of the twelve judges who would decide which city, town, or rural water district would claim bragging rights to the best tap water in the land. It was a subject near and dear to my heart, having once spent a few years living in a farmhouse in Texas—a house my dad claimed had the best-tasting tap water in America. (He might have been right.)

I wasn't content, however, to participate in the competition merely as a judge. I also wanted to enter the contest, and Jeanne Mozier, the tireless and gracious organizer of the event, obliged my whim. I couldn't enter the Texas water because my dad had recently sold the place. I could, however, enter the tap water from my new home in Centreville, Virginia. Centreville had unusually good water, and the nice folks at the Fairfax County Water Authority informed me that the source spring was none other than the

Potomac River at Great Falls. This all sounded too fun to pass up, so I filled my requisite two, one-gallon jugs and brought them to the festival to see how my water stacked up in the rigorous, four-hour taste test.

During those four hours, my esteemed colleague judges and I sampled municipal water from such exotic places as Milford, Delaware; Vancouver, Washington; Augusta, Georgia; Cleveland, Ohio; Baltimore, Maryland; Washington, D.C.; and Richmond, Virginia, to name a few cities. When it was all said and drunk, the winner was Atlantic City, New Jersey. Obvious jokes aside, Atlantic City's water was incredibly sweet and smooth, something that has to do with the sandy soils and percolation patterns of the Atlantic Coastal Plain.

While Atlantic City took the top prize, to my amazement Centreville, Virginia, placed second. Of course, a minor controversy erupted once it was known that the water was submitted by one of the judges. Even the Washington Times *and the* Washington Post *got in on the investigation. In the end, however, all was proven kosher, and I walked away with the second-place honors, fair and square.

I probably would have been harassed even more had my water finished first. Sometimes it pays to be No. 2.

columned facade is draped by the flags of Maryland, District of Columbia, West Virginia, Virginia, Tennessee, and Kentucky, all of which have some family connection to proprietor Jack Barker. Comfortable rooms, many with brass beds, are available in the main house (more like a mansion), while an adjoining modern brick addition houses more contemporary-style digs. No matter where you bunk, you're but a few steps to the Renaissance Spa, where a certified staff will lead you through a choice of whirlpool baths, deep-muscle massages, European-style facials, manicures, and pedicures. If you're looking for a little lifestyle adjustment, the inn's diet center offers personal counseling and courses in nutrition and heart-healthy cooking. You may want to hold off on the diet center until after you've had a chance to sample the fare in the two dining rooms. A good choice is the Steak Dianne, prepared next to your table, and a glass of West Virginia wine. The Country Inn is open year-round. Lodging, spa, and dining rates are moderate. Major credit cards are accepted. Call (304) 258–2210.

There was a time when small-town America had real movie houses—theaters that were destinations in themselves, not just places where films were screened. Berkeley Springs has such a venue in the **Star Theatre** on Washington Street. Besides first-run films, the vintage 1930s movie house features 5-cent candies, popcorn from a 1940s hot-oil popping machine, fresh-pressed apple cider, and overstuffed couches in the back. Owners Jeanne Mozier and Jack Soronen restored the old theater (originally a car dealership) in 1979 and have since brought more than 1,200 movies to town. Jeanne handles the booking, selecting films she believes represent the small community's taste, including kids' movies, adventures, comedies, and the occasional Merchant–Ivory-type production. Jeanne also presides over a preshow lecture on polite theater behavior. Projectionist Jack shows films from a 1940s carbon arc projector. Show time is 8:00 P.M. Friday through Sunday. A Thursday evening show is added from June through September. For feature information or to reserve a couch, call (304) 258–1404.

After the show head down to **Tari's Cafe & Inn,** 123 North Washington, where you can sample outstanding seafood and pastas, enjoy laid-back conversation (this is a local watering hole), and hear some great live blues, rock, folk, and mountain music. The linguini here is heavenly and is served with a rich, creamy, white clam sauce. Another favorite is the carbonara supreme, a beautifully presented mix of bacon, fresh tomatoes, and blue cheese, all tossed with homemade fettuccine. On Friday nights there's a seafood fete complete with all-you-can-eat snow crab legs, clam strips, spiced shrimp, and fried fish.

If you're planning to spend a couple of nights in the area, reserve a private room at the inn, which sits above the restaurant in this double townhouse building. Tari's "sleep and dine" special for two ($129) covers any two nights and includes a lunch and a dinner. The cozy, loftlike rooms have private baths but no phones and are within close walking distance to all Berkeley Springs attractions. Single-night stays start as low as $40. The restaurant opens daily at 11:30 A.M. (noon on Sundays), with lunch lasting until 5:00 P.M. and dinner, 9:00 P.M. The bar typically stays open until 2:00 A.M. Call (304) 258–1196 for dining and room reservations.

Berkeley Springs is a veritable gold mine for antiques and craft collectors, with more than a dozen shops, studios, and consignment centers located within the central business district. These and other outlying boutiques are featured every August in the *Craft Studio and Interior Show,* a three-day affair that lets you see firsthand how local artisans create jewelry, pottery, stained glass, and furniture. The festival's headquartered at the Country Inn. For more information call (304) 258–2210.

The *Old Factory Antique Mall,* 112 Williams Street, feels more like a hands-on museum than a store. Old records, postcards, furniture, toys, jewelry, and books are spread throughout the expansive former factory building, filling every possible nook and cranny. It's a stop that requires at least an hour's worth of browsing and perhaps more if you're doing serious shopping or getting helplessly drawn in by an old baseball card collection or a set of 1950s road maps. The Old Factory is open daily 10:00 A.M. to 5:00 P.M. Call (304) 258–1788 for more information.

Bottling water may not be all that new of a concept—after all, the Egyptians were doing it on the Nile back in the days of the great pharaohs—but it's an idea that's taking off in this country, much to the delight of Berkeley Springs's *West Virginia Spring House Water.* Just a short walk from the Old Factory, at 106 Howard Street, this twenty-year-old bottling company has seen its home and office business balloon in recent years, with a market that saturates the mid-Atlantic states and extends all the way down to hurricane-damaged South Florida. Spring House gathers its water from the nearby springs at Berkeley Springs State Park, filling two tanker cars a day, according to owner Reynolds Hill. "We're tapping into some pretty historic water; water that's good for the body and good for our economy," adds Hill. For special arrangements to tour the plant or sample the product, call Hill and company at (304) 258–2400.

Tari's may have the best linguini in the Eastern Panhandle, but our choice for the best spaghetti and chicken cacciatore goes hands down to *Maria's Garden and Inn,* 201 Independence Street. Tucked away in a historic home (and adjoining building that used to be a mechanic's garage), Maria's now operates as a full bed-and-breakfast and is run by Peg and Jim Perry. The Perrys made their mark on Berkeley Springs by running a popular family restaurant, Perry's Pizza, from 1971 to 1982. Today their inn and restaurant is somewhat of a local institution and is fast gaining the attention of discerning diners and lodgers from

Berkeley Castle

the Washington-Baltimore area. Complementing the pasta dishes is a range of delicious regional favorites like homemade crab cakes and rolled, stuffed sole.

Eating here can be a somewhat spiritual experience—one that extends beyond the food. All three dining rooms are decorated with replicas and paintings of apparitions of the Virgin Mary from around the world. Embedded in the restaurant's stone-wall entrance way, for example, is a reproduction of the Miraculous Cloth of Our Lady of Guadalupe portrait, which has hung in the Basilica in Mexico City for more than 450 years. For those too stuffed to leave, Maria's has eight guest rooms done up in a country chic decor. A first-floor suite comes with a second bedroom and kitchenette. Room rates start at $45 for a single and $70 for the suite. The inn is open year-round, but be sure to make advance reservations for the busy spring and fall months. Travelers should also note that the restaurant is closed on Wednesday. For more information call (304) 258–2021.

On your way out of Berkeley Springs on Route 9 West, you might elect to pay a visit to two other famous landmarks—the *Castle* (304–258–3274) and *Coolfont Resort* (304–258–4500). Hugging the side of Warm Springs Ridge, the native-stone replica of England's Berkeley Castle was built in 1885 by Colonel Samuel Taylor Suit as a wedding gift to his bride, Rosa Pelham, twenty-nine years his junior. After Suit died three years later, Rosa took to the social circuit in earnest, draining her husband's fortune on lavish parties. On the verge of the wrecking ball in 1959, the neglected home was purchased by its present owner, Walter Bird, refurbished, and turned into one of the Mountain State's most visible attractions.

Coolfont, located 5 miles off Route 9 on Cold Valley Road, is the spa of choice among the Washington stress set. Former drug czar William Bennett kicked his cigarette habit here, and Vice President Gore has been a loyal customer for years, even once setting off a minipanic by getting lost in the woods with Tipper! Owners Martha and Sam Ashelman claim the incident, which made international news, was blown out of proportion by the press. The Gores, they say, were simply taking their time exploring the woods.

Back on Route 9, the road winds up to the 1,000-foot summit of **Prospect Peak.** A scenic overlook extends a three-state view of the Cacapon and

Deer Crossing

*A*ll roads may not lead to Paw Paw, but the Potomac River sure does. After spending the better part of the day touring the shops and sights of Berkeley Springs, I headed down to Paw Paw, the town with the funny name I'd never visited before. My knowledge of the tiny Morgan County community was limited to a couple of basic facts. It was home to the "Paw Paw Bends," a great fishing stretch of the Potomac. Paw Paw was also home to a great Appalachian string band that I once had the pleasure of listening to down at the Clifftop Festival in Southern West Virginia, but whose name had long escaped me.

Everything in Paw Paw revolves around the river, so naturally this is where I found myself as nightfall began to descend over the mountains. It was on these muddy banks that I witnessed one of the most peculiar sights in all of my

travels through West Virginia. Looking across the river into Maryland, I saw a deer emerge from a stand of sycamores and leap into the placid waters.

The river, while narrow and calm, was running high from the spring rains, and the buck soon began drifting in the current downstream. Graceful and unfazed, the deer spent the next three minutes or so diligently making his 250-foot crossing. He finally emerged on the West Virginia side before disappearing into an early dusk fog. The faint sound of crackling branches reassured me that he had made his passage unscathed.

As I walked back to my car, an older woman fishing from the shore looked over to me and said, "I guess that ol' boy wanted to be a Mountaineer real bad."

I can't say I blamed him.

Potomac River Valleys. The vista was described by *National Geographic* magazine as one of America's "outstanding beauty spots."

That delicious aroma in the air is coming from directly across the road at ***Panorama Steak House,*** formerly a private club that now serves some rather intimidating beef dishes, including a twenty-four-ounce prime rib and a fourteen-ounce New York strip. If you have an aversion to red meat, don't fret: The Panorama crab cakes, crab Norfolk, and crab imperial, made with fresh Chesapeake Bay blue crabs, are all outstanding, as is the vegetarian pasta. The meal is only half the treat, though. The sunset views from here are breathtaking, and the restaurant has a fascinating history.

The original stone-and-wood building was constructed in 1929 and its interior wooden beams, booths, and wall decor were made from all seventeen different hardwoods found in West Virginia. The fireplace, which is kept burning most of the year, is made from local Oriskany sandstone. Don't worry if you walk up and find the front door locked. Simply ring the buzzer and they'll let you in. It's all part of a tradition that goes back to the days when the Panorama was a private drinking establishment, kind of like a speakeasy, and you had to buzz to get in. Meals are priced moderately and major credit cards are accepted. The restaurant is open from 4:00 P.M. to 9:00 P.M., Tuesday through Friday; 11:00 A.M. to 10:00 P.M., Saturday and Sunday. For reservations call (304) 258-9370.

A fitting final detour in the Eastern Panhandle is to trek west over Great Cacapon Mountain to the little town of **Paw Paw,** the region's westernmost point. Like so many towns in the Eastern Panhandle, Paw Paw lies along the Potomac River and was once a vital rail center. It's named for an unusual fruit tree common to this area. Most of the current 650 residents are direct descendants of the town's original settlers—folks who tamed the river and harvested timber from the surrounding virgin forests. There's not a lot of tourism here save for outstanding river fishing and exploring the ***Paw Paw Tunnel,*** a $1/2$-mile-long mountain tunnel carved by engineers in the mid-1800s during the construction of the Chesapeake & Ohio Canal connecting Washington, D.C., to Cumberland, Maryland. Although named after the West Virginia village, the tunnel is actually across the river in Maryland. It's open year-round to hikers and bikers. Paw Paw's lone lodging option is the **Paw Paw Patch B & B,** a rather basic but comfortable home with three guest rooms. Rates are inexpensive. Call (304) 947-7496.

PLACES TO STAY IN THE EASTERN PANHANDLE

HARPERS FERRY
Harpers Ferry Guest House
Bed and Breakfast,
800 Washington Street;
(304) 535-6955

Hilltop House, 400 East
Ridge Street;
(800) 338-8319

SHEPHERDSTOWN
Bavarian Inn and Lodge,
Route 480, at the Potomac
River; (304) 876-2551

CHARLES TOWN
Towne House Motor Lodge,
549 East Washington
Street; (304) 725-8441

The Carriage Inn Bed and
Breakfast, 417 East Wash-
ington Street;
(304) 728-8003

MARTINSBURG
Hampton Inn, 975 Foxcroft
Avenue; (304) 267-2900

Days Inn, 209 Viking Way;
(304) 263-1800;
www.travelwv.com

Holiday Inn, 301 Foxcroft;
(304) 267-5500

Aspen Hall Inn, 405 Boyd
Avenue; (304) 263-4385

BERKELEY SPRINGS
Cacapon Resort State Park,
U.S. 522, south of Berkeley
Springs; (304) 258-1022

Aaron's Acre Bed and
Breakfast, 501 Johnson Mill
Road; (304) 258-4079

Coolfont Resort, State
Route 9, west of Berkeley
Springs; (304) 258-4500

PLACES TO EAT IN THE EASTERN PANHANDLE
(ALL AREA CODES 304)

HARPERS FERRY
Hilltop House, 400 Ridge
Street; 535-2132

The Anvil Restaurant, 1270
Washington Street;
535-2582

SHEPHERDSTOWN
Bavarian Inn and Lodge,
Route 480 (adjacent to
Potomac River Bridge);
876-2551

The Old Pharmacy cafe and
Soda Fountain, 131 West
German Street; 876-3704

MARTINSBURG
Pulpit & Palette Inn, 516
West John Street; 263-7012

Market House Grill, 100
North Queen Street;
263-7615

Heatherfields Restaurant
(Holiday Inn), 301 Foxcroft
Avenue; 267-5500

Blue Ridge Outlet Center,
315 West Stephen Street;
263-7467

BERKLEY SPRINGS
LaFonte, 116 Fairfax Street;
258-1357

Coolfont Resort and Spa,
1777 Cold Run Valley;
258-8426

Cacapon Resort State Park,
U.S. Route 522 (1 mile
south of town); 258-1022

FOR MORE INFORMATION

Travel Berkley Springs;
(304) 258-9147

Jefferson County
Convention and Visitors
Bureau; (304) 535-2627

Martinsburg/Berkley
County Convention and
Visitors Bureau;
(304) 264-8801

The Potomac Highlands

West Virginia's grand Potomac Highlands region is the state's premier natural area, with an awesome landscape of rugged mountains, pristine rivers, secluded canyons, unusual ecosystems, and seemingly endless forests.

Sparsely populated and largely unspoiled, the Highlands stretch from north to south along the dramatic uplift of the Alleghany Mountains and Plateau, encompassing the counties of Hampshire, Mineral, Hardy, Grant, Tucker, Randolph, Pendleton, Pocahontas, Webster, and Greenbrier. Despite the imposing terrain, the mountain roads here are well maintained, safe (assuming that you watch your speed!), and perfect for relaxed and scenic touring.

Before venturing off the beaten path, be sure to check your fuel tank because gas stations aren't nearly as plentiful here as they are in the Eastern Panhandle and other portions of the state. When in the backcountry, especially at dusk, keep a watchful eye out for deer and bear on the road.

The Allegheny Foothills

The Allegheny Foothills region is located directly west of the Eastern Panhandle. It contains Hampshire, Mineral, Grant, and Hardy Counties, among the prettiest jurisdictions in West Virginia. Although decidedly mountainous, the landscape here is still gentler than other parts of the Potomac Highlands.

A good place to begin a tour of the Allegheny Foothills is in the Hampshire County town of **Romney,** the oldest incorporated city in West Virginia. From Paw Paw, in the Eastern Panhandle, allow about a forty-minute drive down the winding Cacapon and North River Valleys and then another fifteen minutes west on U.S. 50. Romney's graceful Federal-style architecture, with homes and commercial buildings dating back to the mid-1700s, stands in stark contrast to the rugged surrounding terrain of mountains and rocky pastures. This becomes quite

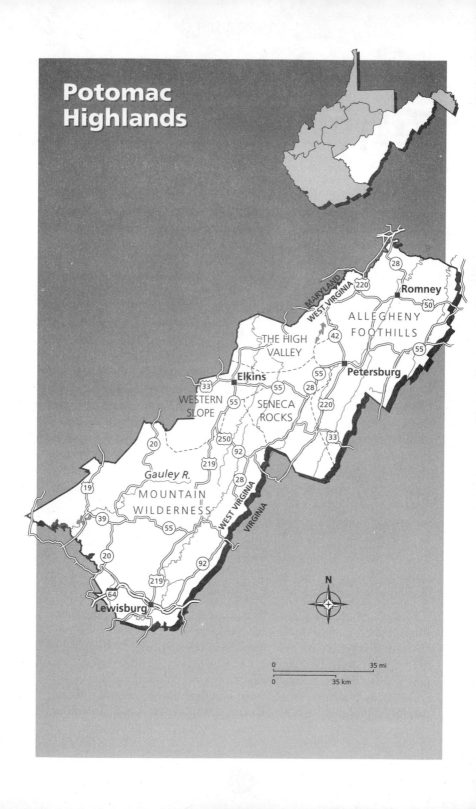

Potomac Highlands

ALLEGHENY
FOOTHILLS

MARYLAND
WEST VIRGINIA

THE HIGH
VALLEY

Elkins

WESTERN
SLOPE

SENECA
ROCKS

Petersburg

Romney

Gauley R.

MOUNTAIN
WILDERNESS

WEST VIRGINIA
VIRGINIA

Lewisburg

N

0   35 mi
0   35 km

Best Annual Events in the Potomac Highlands (All area codes 304)

evident as you head 4 miles north of town on Route 28 to *Crystal Valley Ranch*, a 460-acre horse farm.

Here you're back in the wilderness, and there's no better way to savor the solitude than on the back of one of the ranch's trail horses. Crystal Valley's attentive staff will arrange trips according to your needs, whether it's an hour-long solo journey (with guide) or an all-day group outing up in the hills. The ranch also will arrange for a variety of camping, hiking, and backpacking trips. Fees tend to vary with the activity, but for less than $50 a day you can certainly rid yourself of the city-slicker blues. Crystal Valley Ranch is open year-round, weather permitting. For more information call (304) 822–7444 or (304) 298–3543.

After a night or two in the West Virginia woods, you're bound to feel like a frontiersman (or frontierswoman). To get a feel for the real McCoy, head north on Route 28 to *Fort Ashby*. This eighteenth-century relic of frontier life gives visitors an all-too-real look at how vulnerable settlers were to Indian attack. In fact, the fort is named for Colonel John Ashby, who barely escaped a raid here during the French and Indian War.

Fasnacht, Helvetia; first weekend in February; 924–9019

International Ramp Cook-Off, Elkins; late April; 636–2717

Pioneer Days in Pocahontas County, Marlinton; mid-July; 799–6569

West Virginia Poultry Festival, Moorefield; late July; 538–2725

Augusta Festival, Elkins; early August; 637–1209

Mountain State Forest Festival, Elkins; late September through early October; 636–1824

Potomac Eagle Fall Scenic Rail Excursions, Romney; through October; 422–6069

The large log structure was built in 1755 on the order of George Washington as one of a chain of sixty-nine forts built to defend the Virginia frontier. Made from hand-hewn logs, it centers around a massive chimney that's 14 feet wide and 4 feet thick. Much of the original interior woodwork and wrought iron, including the hinges on the doors, is still intact. After the French and Indian War, Fort Ashby was turned into a schoolhouse. It was restored and opened to the public on July 4, 1939.

The fort is located on Route 46, just inside the town limits of Fort Ashby. Visitors must call ahead to arrange tours. Admission is free, but donations are accepted and appreciated. Call (304) 298–3319, 3926, 3318, or 3722 for more information.

About 12 miles southwest of Fort Ashby on Route 46 sits the quiet, riverside town of Keyser. Built along a hillside that slopes down to the Potomac River (which is very turbulent here), the Victorian-tinged town makes for a great stopping-off point for tired and hungry travelers. A great spot to unwind is the lovely **Candlewyck Inn,** 65 South

Don't Feed the Bears

*N*ot too long after we first fell for each other, we fell for West Virginia. After moving as newlyweds to Northern Virginia, our long weekend drives quickly found us in some magical places in the Mountain State.

After only a few weekend trips, we decided we needed a piece of it to call our own. After scanning the papers for some weeks, we found our own little bit of heaven in the form of 5 acres on Short Mountain, in Hampshire County. We didn't have much of a view, but we had a little stream, a flat place to build, and grand images of the cabin we would someday put there.

Because we couldn't wait to accumulate enough wealth to put a roof over our patch of ground, we decided to camp on it whenever we could. Camping there was very important to us because as apartment dwellers we needed to feel connected to our only asset! So, every once in a while we'd pack up our tiny urban car with every bit of camping gear we owned and head "to the land."

Steve was always much more at ease there than was I. I don't know if it's gender or youthful camping experiences that make the difference, but I was always pretty jittery on the land once night fell. We had a few neighbors along the roughly 1-mile-long stretch of gravel road than ran straight to the top of the mountain, and some of them were permanent. Still, though, I relied heavily on my dog, a lab mix named Dewey, and my husband to warn me of any danger.

The last time I ever camped there was in early fall, just before cold weather set in. We had set up camp, and it was about dusk. Steve had built a roaring fire, the tent was pitched, mountain music was playing, and a peaceful evening was in progress. I decided to go to "the ladies room" one last time before it got completely dark, so I walked a short distance into the gloom of the woods to do so. Right as I began my task, I heard a great crashing through the trees on my right. It was some distance away, it was big, and it was coming fast. I put myself back together and ran back to Steve, saying, "there's something coming, and it's big!"

He didn't move. He said something along the lines of "you're just spooked, and it's just your imagination," but I held fast to my story. We never saw what it was; perhaps it saw our fire, or heard or saw us, and didn't come any closer. After a while, because I was so unnerved, we drove to a motel to spend the night and came back the next day for our gear.

Some weeks later, when Steve was up there camping with one of our friends, he ran into a neighbor, a year-round resident, and asked him if he'd ever seen any bears on our property. "Oh yes, we see them all the time. . . . They come to eat the hickory nuts right under that big tree where your tent is now."

Somehow, I had a lot more credibility after that.

Mineral Street, which is perched in the middle of Keyser's historic district a few blocks up the river. With its inviting Victorian facade and comfortable modern rooms, the Candlewyck offers a bit of luxury amid the rugged surroundings of the North Branch Valley. The dining room, which is open daily from 4:00 P.M. to 1:00 A.M., tempts travelers with hearty charbroiled steaks and fresh Maryland seafood delicacies like Chesapeake Bay crab cakes and oysters. Each guest room comes with a private bath, two telephones, and color television. Rates begin at $50 and include a delicious country breakfast. Colorful antiques and curio shops along Mineral and Main Streets are just a short stroll away.

The area west of Fort Ashby and Keyser, along the banks of the North Branch of the Potomac River, was once one of intense surface coal mining, or, in the uglier vernacular, "strip mining." Although mining has kept the region somewhat economically viable, it has laid a heavy hand on its ecosystem. During heavy rains and river flooding—an all-too-common occurrence here—the abandoned coal mines fill with water and then ultimately release a toxic acidic runoff into the fragile Potomac, killing fish and plant life in its wake.

During the early 1970s visionaries from the U.S. Army Corps of Engineers decided to construct a special lake to control flooding and environmental degradation. The result is *Jennings Randolph Lake,* a 1,000-acre impoundment on the Potomac River bordering Maryland and West Virginia. It's located about 27 miles southwest of Fort Ashby on Route 46. The lake acts as a receptacle for acid runoff and stabilizes the water downstream by periodically releasing pure water from the dam. The result is cleaner water in the lake and the river. The project has become so successful that brown trout, all but depleted during the 1970s, are now spawning in the tailwaters below the dam.

Aside from the environmental good stewardship, the lake has become a major recreational mecca for boaters, anglers, and campers. An interesting geological feature found near the lake's visitor center is *Waffle Rock,* a sandstone structure with a geometrical pattern resembling that of a waffle, the result of nearly 300 million years of folding, fracturing, and weathering. The lake facilities are open year-round. For more information call (301) 359–3861.

South of the lake, on the eastern slope of Saddle Mountain in Mineral County, sits a small, unassuming cabin that was the birthplace of Nancy Hanks, mother of Abraham Lincoln. The sparse wooden structure was built in the late 1700s from native hardwoods the Hanks family cleared to farm the hollow. The cabin and surrounding hardscrabble pastures and woodlands are now part of the *Nancy Hanks Memorial,* a state park facility open to the public year-round from dawn to dusk. It is yet another reminder that seeds of greatness are often sown in the most humble of places. There is no admission charge for the area, but getting there can be tricky. From Route 50, your best bet is to head south on Maysville Road toward the small farming community of Antioch. About 3 miles beyond Antioch, look for a brown state historic site sign on the right-hand side of the road. Head west about 2 miles to the cabin.

If you're still feeling adventurous, continue on Maysville Road about 10 miles and turn west onto Greenland Gap Road. This short but spectacular 4-mile stretch of road is home to the *Greenland Gap Nature Preserve,* part of the Nature Conservancy's effort to save unspoiled wilderness. In season you'll see spectacular rhododendron blooms, and any time of the year you can catch glimpses of the mountain gap's huge limestone walls, pristine creeks and waterfalls, and perhaps a bobcat or a black bear and her cub. In the warm months park your car alongside the creek and go for a wade in these gin-clear waters. Chances are you can spend an hour up on the gap and not see or hear another soul pass by. The Mineral County preserve is open year-round from dawn to dusk, and there is no admission charge.

In neighboring Hardy County, down in the bucolic South Branch Valley, be sure to stop by *Old Fields Church,* the second-oldest house of worship in the state. It's located just off U.S. 220, about 3 miles north of Moorefield. The church was built in 1812 and was known at that time as the Fort Pleasant Meeting House. The small redbrick and tin-roof building was used by both Methodists and Presbyterians for more than 100 years. It also was reported to be the first schoolhouse in West Virginia. A few years ago the church was headed for the wrecker's ball before a local preservation group stepped in and began renovations. It's now owned by the Duffey Memorial United Methodist Church. Occasional services and social gatherings are still held here. Call (304) 538–6560 for more information.

Fewer than five minutes away, in the sleepy and scenic town of Moorefield, is a bed-and-breakfast so steeped in history and so elegantly appointed that it's worth an overnight stop on anyone's busy vacation itinerary. *The McMechen House Inn* is a three-story Greek Revival–style mansion situated in the center of Moorefield's historic district. The 142-year-old house was the home of S. A. McMechen, a local merchant and political activist. During the Civil War, the house periodically served as headquarters to both the Union and Confederate forces as military control of the South Branch Valley changed hands.

THE POTOMAC HIGHLANDS

The valley, by the way, contains one of the nation's highest concentrations of antebellum homes, and the McMechen House is one of the few in the area open to the public.

After you've peeked into the mansion's six guest rooms, parlor, and porches, take a short stroll down to the South Branch of the Potomac River, which winds lazily through this Mayberry-esque town of 2,000 people. Bring your fishing pole or enjoy a languid canoe ride. If you want to stay dry, wander in and out of the district's antiques shops. Whatever you do be sure to make it back to the inn for afternoon tea, a great time to converse with other travelers and your hosts, Bob and Linda Curtis. Rates here range from $55 to $65 for one person, $65 to $75 for two. Credit cards are accepted, but cash or traveler's checks are preferred. Sorry, no pets or children under twelve (without prior arrangement). The inn is open year-round. To make reservations call (800) 2–WVA–Inn.

BEST ATTRACTIONS IN THE POTOMAC HIGHLANDS (ALL AREA CODES 304)

The Greenbrier Resort,
White Sulphur Springs;
536–1110

Blackwater Outdoor Center,
Davis; 259–5117

Elk River Touring Center,
Slatyfork; 572–3771

Canaan Valley Resort State Park,
Davis; 866–4121

Snowshoe Mountain Resort,
Snowshoe; 572–1000

Blackwater Falls,
Davis; 259–5216

Seneca Rocks National Recreation Area,
Seneca Rocks; 567–2827

When it comes to water quality, scenery, and isolation, few parts of the country can claim as many ideal canoeing waters as the Mountain State. *Eagle's Nest Outfitters* is the premier canoe rental and river vacation-planning company on the South Branch of the Potomac. It's located outside of Petersburg, on U.S. 220. Here, in the shadows of some of the highest peaks in West Virginia, anglers, campers, and canoeists from all over the United States come to experience more than 80 miles of virtually untouched rivers. Eagle's Nest experts can arrange group outings or tailor trips to individual tastes. There are eight different single-day trips of varying length and difficulty and several two-to-five-day trips also are available.

For those in search of exciting white water, try rafting through the isolated *Smoke Hole Canyon.* The Lower Smoke Hole Canyon trip begins with breathtaking views of Cave Mountain and Eagle Rock, giant granite and limestone outcroppings that tower more than 100 feet above the river. Milder waters can be found by planning a trip through The Trough, a 3-mile-long canyon featuring a stunning 1,000-foot wall along one section. The majestic setting is made even more dramatic by the dozen or so American bald eagles that inhabit the area and are regularly sighted from the river.

If you're more interested in baiting a hook than paddling, Eagle's Nest also plans fishing trips. Hundreds of trophy-sized small- and large-mouth bass, catfish, and trout are landed each year on the productive South Branch. Canoeing and fishing trip reservations must be made by phone or by mail three weeks in advance for holidays and weekends. Prices start as low as $20 a day per canoe. That includes canoe, paddles, life jackets, shuttle service, safety lectures, and instructions. Eagle's Nest is open daily from April 1 through October 31. Call (304) 257–2393 for information.

Double Eagles

*A*s stressed-out urbanites we saved as many free weekends as possible for touring West Virginia. We often took friends with us to camp, hike, canoe or just enjoy the gorgeous, peaceful countryside.

On one occasion, Steve and I and two other adventurous companions, John, an old friend from our newspaper days in Texas, and his girlfriend, Deborah, came along to canoe with us. We had previously traversed the South Branch of the Potomac River, which flowed near our land, and were completely enthralled by the scenery along the way. We wanted to share it with our buddies, so we invited them to get out of Washington, D.C., for the weekend and come along.

We hooked up with Eagles Nest Outfitters in Petersburg, who took us to the spot where we put in. It was a perfect weekend. It was early fall, and the air was crisp and the sky deepest blue. The leaves were starting to turn, lending their glorious colors to our trip. The water was almost kelly green and so clear that sitting in the red canoe, we could see schools of bass cruise by, even catfish sitting on the bottom. In places, the water was wide and boulder-strewn, and a black and red "leaf peeper" train crossed above us as we drifted past wide, green cow pastures on either side of the river.

We stopped and ate lunch on a wide sandbar and watched a few fellow canoers drift by while our dog, Dewey, splashed in the shallows.

In one section of the trip, called "The Trough" because of the steepness of the valley that the river flows through, we were silent, looking up at the great cliffs rising above us. Suddenly, out from a craggy tree growing in the rocks near the top, a bald eagle flew into view. It was huge, beautiful, and majestic. It was also so close! Soon there were two, alternately soaring and diving for fish. We were silent, stunned. Our friend, John, said he was so moved, he almost stood up and saluted. It was an amazing sight. As we drifted out from under them, we turned to watch them for as long as we could, until a bend in the river removed them from view.

I have since been on several canoe trips, but none will ever top that one in my memory and in my heart.

As you wend your way south on U.S. 220 from Petersburg, you'll pass a small white country store about 6 miles down the road. Throughout your ramblings in West Virginia, you'll pass hundreds like this, but make no mistake—this one is different. This is the **Country Store Opry,** a grocery that doubles as a live bluegrass and old-time music venue. Old-fashioned hoedowns, featuring local banjo, mountain dulcimer, fiddle, and guitar players, are held in back of the store every first, third, and fifth Saturday night from April through October. These unpretentious gatherings, sometimes called "front-porchers" by West Virginians, often showcase some of the best mountain music ever made and are an integral part of the cultural fabric of Appalachia.

Admission to the Country Store Opry is $1.50 for adults, free for children under twelve. For reservations and information call (304) 257–1743.

Seneca Rocks

Named after the imposing sandstone spirals that tower high above the South Branch Valley, the Seneca Rocks region encompasses Pendleton and parts of Grant and Randolph Counties. The deep gorges, jutting rock formations, wild rivers, and arching mountains (including the highest point in the state—4,861-foot Spruce Knob) make for perhaps the most spectacular natural scenery in all of West Virginia.

Born of Mother Earth's violent upheaval 185 million years ago, **Smoke Hole Gorge,** running mostly parallel with U.S. 220 in Grant and Pendleton Counties, is one of the most remote and beautiful areas in the United States. Most people don't know that, because it's nearly impossible to get to. But it can be done.

Smoke Hole is where the South Branch of the Potomac River squeezes between North Fork Mountain and Cave Mountain, creating spectacular waterfalls, sluices, and white-water conditions. These raging waters have formed caves, carved canyons, and shaped the wild landscape in an extraordinary fashion. An ever-present fog through the "hole" makes visitors feel like they're in a bygone era. It's easy to believe the old myths here. Earliest settlers said the "smoke" came from a moonshiner's still. Some claimed it came from Indian fires.

Smoke Hole is managed by the **Monongahela National Forest** as part of the Spruce Knob–Seneca Rocks National Recreation Area. It's a hunting, fishing, hiking, canoeing, and camping paradise. The easiest access into the gorge is via Route 2, near Upper Tract, a tiny town 18 miles southwest of Petersburg along U.S. 220. Route 2 parallels the river into the canyon for about 8 miles. On the way in you'll see a few fishermen and perhaps a canoeist or two.

After 8 miles the paved road ends at a junction featuring an old country store and a log church. One fork of the road continues along the river, the other rises to the north of the shoulder of North Fork Mountain and down to Route 28. If you take the "high road," notice the small farms nestled in the hollows and the abandoned log cabins decorating the clearings. Traffic is almost nonexistent, so you might want to stop along the way for an impromptu picnic.

If you decide to spend the night, there are some outstanding places to sleep under the stars. The largest is the Big Bend Campground, with forty-six sites managed by the National Forest Service. It's open April 15 to October 1 (a portion of the campground is open March 1 to December 15, but there you'll have to pump your own water). As the name implies the campground is situated along a huge bend of the river. A traveling buddy from out West who studied astronomy in college claimed he had never witnessed such clear nighttime skies before.

Primitive camping sites are scattered along Smoke Hole Road (Route 28/11) on North Fork Mountain and throughout the backcountry except at trailheads. For camping and other recreation information within the gorge, call the National Forest Service at (304) 257–4488.

Another lodging alternative is the ever obscure and totally unique **Smoke Hole Lodge.** This privately owned red cedar and fieldstone wilderness retreat sits on a 1,500-acre tract of riverfront land inside the gorge. It's located about 12 miles south of Petersburg but cannot be reached without a four-wheel-drive vehicle. The 5-mile "road" is so bumpy that the trek takes nearly ninety minutes. Indeed, you can probably walk it in the same time! This is about as far off the beaten path as it gets, an experience you won't—nor should—ever forget.

There is neither electricity nor telephone here. The lodge runs on kerosene, wood fires, and bottled gas. The great outdoors is the main attraction, and you'll get a healthy dose of it in the form of outstanding smallmouth bass fishing in the river pools in front of the lodge and the miles of hiking trails that meander through the nearby hillsides and woodlands. Accommodations are simple and rustic, with five double bedrooms and two dormitories. Each has a private bathroom. Downstairs you'll find a living room, dining room, kitchen, deck, and two porches. Hearty family-style meals are served in the dining room overlooking the river. Wood-cooked steak and trout dinners are especially memorable.

Gas Mojo

Before we had children (back when time was our own), one of our favorite ways to relax was to go for long, lazy drives in the countryside, despite the fact that our car was roughly half the size of our sofa back home. Many, many weekends found us camping out alongside a rocky river pass or staying in comfortable, yet decidedly downscale accommodations at the foot of a mountain.

On one of these outings, we were driving near Dolly Sods, an unusual geographic area whose rocky Forest Service roads defy most suburban motorists. After winding our way up near the top, we came to a fork in the road. To the right was a sign that pointed the way to Dolly Sods; to the left was an unmarked gravel road. Because I have learned over the years to "go with the flow" when it comes to traveling with Steve, I didn't say a word when he turned left into uncharted territory.

Now I should point out that we had recently found out that we were expecting our first child. That's important because pregnant women are known for two things—nausea and frequent potty stops—neither of which are easily addressed on a mountain road in the middle of the Monongahela National Forest. To compound the situation, I had noticed that we were very low on gas, and I was not in any condition—or mood—to walk. For Steve, seeing how many miles he can eke out before stopping is part of the fun of driving.

We continued on our winding, bumpy descent through clouds of dust. I was getting more and more nervous because the view outside my window was getting darker and darker as the woods surrounding us got more dense. This is big-time bear country, and I didn't relish sitting on the side of the road waiting for someone to find us if we ran out of gas, let alone try to walk out, or down, as the case was.

I rode most of this route tight-lipped and angry. Steve, sensing my annoyance, got defensive and anxious, and all the fun of this drive was about over. At one point, we saw a group of hikers. Steve asked how far to civilization. They replied "not far!" and kept walking uphill. That cheered me considerably.

We kept driving, and driving and driving—the scenery was spectacular. But as I peered through the gloom, I envisioned bears everywhere. I alternately glared at Steve and at the gas gauge, which by now was past "E." Luckily, we were descending at such an angle that we figured we could coast for a long distance, which would be a bonus—possibly.

Finally, after three extremely steep hairpin turns, we dropped down onto a paved road. To our amazement, without any other sign of life in sight, a gas station sat immediately to our left. It was small, it was unpainted, and it only had privies out back, but they had gas! After we filled up, sighed, and made up, we turned back on the paved road only to discover we were just a few miles from our motel room. Steve claims to this day he knew where he was all along, but I say he was just lucky.

He does still have, as we say, "gas mojo," for when he decides to stop for gas, no matter where, a gas station magically appears.

The lodge is open May through October. For fall foliage season book early, perhaps even a year in advance. Daily rates are $90 for one person, $75 for each additional person; rates include round-trip transportation from Petersburg, lodging, linen service, three meals a day, and use of all facilities. For information write to Smoke Hole Lodge, P.O. Box 953, Petersburg, WV 26847.

Just to the west of the Smoke Hole Gorge, off Route 28, about 10 miles south of Petersburg, lies another fascinating natural area, *Dolly Sods.* This 10,215-acre National Wilderness and Scenic Area is characterized by rugged boulder-strewn plains, windswept spruce trees, cool mountain air, and 50-mile vistas.

Dolly Sods was once a forest of giant red spruces and hemlocks, most claiming diameters in excess of 4 feet. These incredible trees were logged in the 1800s, and the hot fires that burned during the logging destroyed the underlying fertile humus layer. About the same time local farmers burned the plains to create grazing land, or sods. One such group of pioneers that cleared the area was the Dahle family. Over the years Dahle somehow became Dolly, as in the present Dolly Sods.

The Sods' plant life and climate are what make it so unusual. It's actually more akin to the boreal forest of northern Canada than it is to any other part of the United States. In the summer azaleas, mountain laurels, rhododendrons, and blueberries thrive despite the infertile soil. Cranberries and insect-eating sundew plants are adjacent to more arid, boulder-strewn, open areas. Northern hardwoods are found in the coves and drainages, and red pines grow in several areas.

Save a little energy and appetite for some *berry picking,* a favorite pastime among visitors and native bears. Blueberries, huckleberries, teaberries, and cranberries blanket the area. Ramps (a very strong wild leek) can be found in moist wooded areas. Take your fare to the shady Dolly Sods picnic area to eat and enjoy the natural surroundings. It's located on Forest Road 19 just south of the scenic area. Picnic tables, grills, and portable toilets are provided.

Dolly Sods has several *hiking trails,* all marked only by ax blazes or rock cairns (mounds). Distances are not indicated. When you're ready to pull off your hiking boots, you can bed down overnight in the area's only campground, Red Creek. It has twelve campsites (two walk-in and ten suitable for trailers). Portable toilets and a water well are provided.

A visit to Dolly Sods is well worth your time, but you should observe a few cautions. Because it sits directly atop the Allegheny Plateau, at elevations

OTHER ATTRACTIONS IN THE
POTOMAC HIGHLANDS

Seneca Caverns—
Riverton

Hillsboro General Store—
Hillsboro

Short Mountain Wildlife
Management Area—
Kirby

Beartown State Park—
Droop

ranging from 2,600 to 4,000 feet, weather can change suddenly. Storms can be severe and life threatening, and dense fogs can confuse even the most experienced outdoorsman or -woman. The area is noted for its fierce westerly winds (note the one-sided red spruce trees); snow in the fall, winter, and spring; and low temperatures during any month of the year. Also be watchful of poisonous snakes. And if that's not enough, be on the lookout for old mortar shells. Yes, mortar shells. The area was used for military exercises during World War II, and some live shells remain. If you come by a shell, don't touch it!

For more information about Dolly Sods, call the National Forest Service at (304) 636–1800, (304) 257–4488, or (304) 567–2827.

Straight down the road (literally) from Dolly Sods are the fabled **Seneca Rocks.** Named for one of the Indian tribes that passed through the area, these sandstone rock formations rise more than 900 feet above the North Fork Valley and Route 28 and U.S. 33. This is one of the most popular rock-climbing areas in the East, and on any given weekend—or weekday for that matter—you'll see cars with license plates from as far away as Vermont, Florida, and Illinois.

If you're brave (or crazy) enough to scale these spirals, look for the words "D. B., September 16, 1908" carved into the top of the south peak. No one is quite sure who D. B. was, although one theory states he may have been D. Bittenger, a civil engineer who surveyed the area for the National Park Service. Whoever he or she was, D. B. beat Paul Brandt, Don Hubbard, and Sam Moore to the top, a trio credited with being the first recorded climbers to master the rocks and reach the summit in 1938.

Since that time thousands of thrill seekers have climbed Seneca Rocks, including members of the Tenth Mountain Division, who trained here during World War II. For those who yearn to see the view from the top but don't want to risk life and limb in the process, there is another way. A steep and relatively safe 1.3-mile, self-guided, interpretive trail ascends the north edge of the rocks to a viewing platform.

If you'd rather keep your feet firmly planted on the ground, there's still plenty to do in the area, starting with a visit to the Seneca Rocks visitors center. Inside you'll find exhibits and a video explaining the history and geology of the area. In the adjacent picnic area, visitors can watch the brave climbers cling precariously to the rocks or stroll down to the South Branch for a bit of catch-and-release trout fishing.

Seneca Rock is open year-round. For more information call the visitors center at (304) 567–2827.

The wild beauty of Seneca Rocks serves as a spectacular backdrop for *Harper's Old Country Store,* a thriving turn-of-the-century retailer that shows no signs of slowing down. It's one of the oldest continuously operated businesses in the state, still run by members of the Harper family.

The wood-frame store was built in 1902 and originally operated under the name of D. C. Harper and Co. Its interior today is much the same as it was then. Inside you'll find groceries, hardware, clothing, snacks, gifts, and hunting and fishing equipment. While you're stocking up, take a look at the store's original board floor, the antique metal-blocked ceiling, and the original shelving and counters. You can't miss the mounted West Virginia black bear, which stands guard over the store's ground floor.

If you're in the mood to eat, step up to **The Front Porch** restaurant, located on the second floor of Harper's. It's nothing fancy, just simple, tasty, and well-prepared food in a casual atmosphere. The view isn't bad either. Try a slice of fresh dough pizza, or sample one of the wheat pita pocket sandwiches. They're good enough to lure you down from the rocks.

Harper's Old Country Store is located at the intersection of Routes 33 and 55 in Seneca Rocks. Store hours are 7:00 A.M. to 8:30 P.M. weekdays and Saturday, and 8:00 A.M. to 8:00 P.M. Sunday. The restaurant is open Saturday from 11:00 A.M. to 10:00 P.M., and Sunday through Friday from 11:00 A.M. to 9:00 P.M. Call (304) 567–2555 for more information.

Now that you're loaded with provisions from Harper's, it's time to explore the state's largest mountain, *Spruce Knob,* and take in what's probably the finest vista in West Virginia. From Seneca Rocks drive 10 miles south on U.S. 33 before taking a right on County Road 3³/₄ (look for the sign to Spruce Knob National Recreation Area). After a mile or so, the paved mountain road will give way to gravel, which will remain this way for the next 8 miles until you reach the summit of the 4,861-foot mountain. Budget ¹/₂ hour to get up the mountain (if you make it quicker than that, you're probably driving too fast) and keep your eyes posted for wildlife that will frequently dart on the road. This isn't a place where you want to apply the brakes quickly; skidding on gravel on a narrow mountain road without guard rails isn't exactly conducive to relaxation.

Once you reach the summit of this gorgeous mountain, you'll be glad you made the trip. Near the top of the mountain, the gravel returns to blacktop and winds around to a parking lot. An easy ½-mile foot trail takes you along the summit ridge, which is sprinkled with massive limestone and granite boulders; windblown, one-sided, red spruce trees; and dense pockets of blueberry, huckleberry, and mountain ash. The trail ends at a two-story observation deck that affords views of more than 75 miles in any direction, including an eastern vista extending all the way to Virginia's Shenandoah Valley.

Harper's Old Country Store

Like the Dolly Sods Wilderness Area, the Spruce Knob region was once farmed by hearty Scottish-Irish and German settlers, and traces of the pastures they forged by clearing timber can still be seen more than a hundred years later. If you plan to camp out, the National Forest Service maintains a forty-three-site Spruce Knob Campground about 3 miles down from the summit, next to Spruce Knob Lake, a 25-acre pond that provides some good trout fishing. Backcountry camping also is allowed throughout Spruce Knob, and the same types of precautions you would take on Dolly Sods should be applied here (see page 41).

The recreation area is open year-round, except during snowy and icy periods when the roads can be life threatening. For more information stop by the Seneca Rock Visitors Center or call (304) 567–2827.

The High Valley

The High Valley region is the area in and around Tucker County's Canaan Valley, pronounced "keh-nane" by West Virginians. It's the highest valley in the East and one of the most peculiar, geologically and geographically speaking, in the United States.

Canaan Valley is a place of quiet beauty where the deer eat out of your hand; where the oranges, reds, and yellows of October are incomparable, and where the lush springs, mild summers, and deep winter snows make the mountain vistas breathtaking. The 3,200-foot-high, 14-mile-long valley is located in Tucker County, near the Maryland border, and is dissected by Route 32.

Portions of Canaan have been designated a National Natural Landmark because of the unusual Canadian forest plant life and the 6,700 acres of fragile upcountry wetlands. The high Allegheny Mountains that rim the valley seem to act as magnets for snow. In fact Canaan receives 150 to 200 inches of the white stuff each year. Late spring snows aren't uncommon. As you might guess the valley has become one of the best ski areas in the Mid-Atlantic, boasting more than a half-dozen resorts, including Canaan Valley State Park, Timberline, and Beaver Ridge.

When the weather warms up, hiking, golfing, and fishing take center stage. Hikers take to the Blackwater/Canaan Trail, an 8-mile mountain path connecting Blackwater Falls State Park to Canaan Valley State Park. In early March trout fishing heats up on the tea-colored Blackwater River and stays hot through the summer months. For those who'd rather swing a club than a fly rod, the eighteen-hole championship golf course at Canaan Valley State Park (800–CALL–WVA) offers a great summertime escape.

At the northern edge of Canaan Valley sits the eclectic little town of Davis. Looking a bit like the fictional Cicely, Alaska, of television's *Northern Exposure,* Davis is the highest incorporated town (elevation 3,200 feet) east of the Mississippi. Here you'll find a number of unusual attractions. ***The Art Company of Davis*** is at the top of the list.

This enterprising venture is actually a membership cooperative formed in 1990 by a small group of local artisans as a forum to exhibit work and stimulate creativity. Today that group has grown to more than 100 artists who produce both contemporary and traditional arts and crafts. Their wares are housed in a turn-of-the-century, 8,000-square-foot frame building located right on Route 32 next to the Davis Post Office. Interestingly enough, the blue wooden building was once the company store for the Babcock Lumber and Boom Company.

All of the art work, including wood carvings, textiles, and oil paintings depicting outdoor life in the region, are juried for quality and originality. Visitors to the company can pick up paintings, toys, quilts, pottery, baskets, rugs, musical instruments, photographs, furniture, and books on West Virginia crafts and culture.

The Art Company is open Tuesday through Saturday, 10:00 A.M. to 6:00 P.M., and Sunday, 11:00 A.M. to 5:00 P.M. For more information call (304) 259–4218.

Almost directly across the street from the gallery is **Bright Morning,** a bed-and-breakfast that was once a boardinghouse for itinerant lumberjacks. Proprietors George and Missy Bright restored the wood-frame building to include seven bedrooms and one suite, all with private baths. Breakfast is provided to all guests. Reservations are suggested for lunch and dinner, which typically feature local fish, meats, and produce prepared in a "country gourmet" fashion. Bright Morning also has a gift shop, Brightest and Best, which stocks beautiful gifts that are hand-made by local artists. The inn is open year-round. Rates range from $55 to $65 for double occupancy. Call (304) 259–5119.

The Western Slope

The Western Slope of the Allegheny Mountains shows its face in Randolph County, where the hills tend to come down on top of one another, adding to the mythical spirit of the place. The remoteness of the land only seems to intensify the friendliness of the people who live here.

From Davis follow U.S. 219 south through the Monongahela National Forest to Elkins, the Randolph County seat. This is the home of the **Augusta Heritage Center,** a haven for traditional Appalachian music, crafts, dancing, and folklore.

The world-renowned musical performance and craft-learning center was founded in 1973 on the secluded, tree-lined campus of Davis & Elkins College. Its guiding mission is to keep the spirit of West Virginia's mountain culture alive by sharing it with natives and visitors alike. It's been a huge success. Each July and August hundreds of students from across North America descend on Elkins to take part in Augusta's intimate workshops taught by master artists and musicians. Courses range from fiddle and banjo instruction to log-house building, Celtic stone carving, and African-American storytelling.

August also ushers in the Augusta Festival in Elkins City Park, a weekend celebration of free concerts, juried craft fairs, children's art and music exhibitions, dancing, food, and storytelling. The Spring Dulcimer

Festival in April and the Fiddler's Reunion and Old-Time Week in October are homecomings of sorts for mountain musicians from throughout the United States and from as far away as Nova Scotia, Ireland, and Scotland.

For more information on courses and programs provided by the Augusta Heritage Center, call (304) 636–1903.

If your travels haven't yet taken you to Europe, you can at least get a glimpse of what one European country must be like with a visit to the Randolph County community of *Helvetia.* This hidden village, tucked into the folds of the Alleghenies about an hour south of Elkins off U.S. 250, was settled by feisty German and Swiss immigrants in 1869 and today has all the flavor of a true Alpine community. It was the first town district in the state to be placed on the National Register of Historic Places.

Helvetia claims about 200 inhabitants, considerably fewer than the 1,200 or so who populated the village and surrounding hills and hollows around the turn of the century during the area's logging boom. As you stroll the tidy streets, don't be surprised to hear a few residents chatting in their ancestors' native tongue.

It is the native cuisine, however, that keeps many outsiders returning to Helvetia on a regular basis. Find the sign that says *Gruss Gott, tritt ein, bring Cluck herein* (PRAISE GOD, STEP IN, BRING LUCK HEREIN), and you've found *The Hutte* restaurant, known for its locally grown food prepared in Swiss style. It's the hub of activity in Helvetia. Owner Eleanor Mailloux is a descendant of one of Helvetia's original settlers, and she doesn't skimp on authenticity. Menu items include *pfeffernusse,* a ginger cookie; Stout Country Soup, a thick vegetable beef soup; and a locally made cheese. All of this and more is served at Bernerplatte, the Swiss version of Sunday brunch. Other menu items include sauerbraten, bratwurst, homemade sausage, homemade breads, pineapple, and pickled beets. The Hutte is open daily from noon to 7:00 P.M. Call (304) 924–6435.

If you arrive on a weekday and want to stay over for the brunch, ask Eleanor if she has room at the inn. She also owns *The Beekeeper Inn,* (304) 924–6435, a bed-and-breakfast. It's a cozy, four-room affair complete with private baths, a common room overstuffed with books, and a large deck shaded by huge pine trees.

After a sumptuous repast or a long afternoon nap, take a walk around this fairy-tale-like village. Don't miss the flag-bedecked bridge leading to the pottery shop; the Cheese Haus, formerly a working cheese shop; the one hundred-year-old church; and the town museum housed in an original settler's cabin. The latter is filled with interesting artifacts, including the original Swiss flag the settlers brought with them from the old country.

If the Beekeeper is booked for the evening, try nearby *Grandpa John's Country Kitchen & Inn,* halfway between Helvetia and Pickens, a community even smaller than Helvetia. The farmhouse, which now serves as an inn and restaurant, was built by an early Helvetia settler, John J. Betler, in the 1880s. Proprietors Marty and Pat Crumm restored the stone and wooden shingle home in 1989 and now run it as a full bed-and-breakfast. The Crumms also serve a huge Sunday buffet, so if you're a guest, go light on the complimentary breakfast that morning. Grandpa John's is located on Pickens Road, 2½ miles south of Helvetia. The inn, open daily for overnight guests, is also within a few minutes drive of Holly River State Park and Kumbrabow State Forest, two huge natural areas that offer a number of great hiking, fishing, and exploring opportunities. For inn reservations call the Crumms at (304) 924–5503.

Helvetia is no theme park. It's an active community with deep pride in its roots. As such, it celebrates its heritage with several endearing customs and festivals. Hundreds come from far and wide to attend such events as Swiss Independence Day in August, the Helvetia Fair in September, and *Fasnacht,* a Mardi Gras–like fete in February that celebrates the coming of spring. *Fasnacht* participants hang Old Man Winter in effigy and don costumes to "scare away" winter. If visitors arrive without proper costumes, they're encouraged to rummage through local attics to find something fitting to wear. The celebration is usually held the Saturday before Ash Wednesday and is kicked off with a community-wide Swiss feast and an Appalachian music show.

Mountain Wilderness

The Mountain Wilderness region consists of Pocahontas, Greenbrier, Webster, and parts of Randolph Counties. As its name implies, this is the most mountainous part of West Virginia, and it contains the largest swath of the Potomac Highlands.

Any place that's called a "beautiful spot" by someone as noteworthy as American inventor Thomas Edison must be special. The New Jersey–born inventor was referring to West Virginia's *Cheat Mountain Club,* a 103-year-old lodge along the banks of the Shavers Fork River

Spruce Knob, the tallest mountain in West Virginia (over 4,800 feet), marks the geographic center of the Potomac Highlands region.

and high atop the namesake mountain that contains nine of the state's ten tallest peaks.

The lodge and surrounding 180-acre private retreat was built by members of the Cheat Mountain Sportsmen's Association for hunting and other outdoor sports. It's located right off of U.S. 250, about an hour southeast of Helvetia. In 1988 the club was purchased by a group of West Virginians to sponsor the perpetual use and hospitality of this gracious, comfortable lodge. Although Edison, Henry Ford, and Harvey Firestone have been among the lodge's notable guests, you needn't be a millionaire to enjoy its rustic charm.

Guests are pampered with a range of outdoor activities, from horseback riding and canoeing to fishing and swimming in one of the large pools on Shavers Fork. Inside, the hand-hewn spruce log interior exudes comfort and warmth, as does the constantly burning fire in the stone fireplace. Cheat Mountain's legendary dining room serves three family-style meals daily on the lodge's original china. Personal menu requests also are prepared, but you won't want to miss any of the specialties, including a full-course country breakfast, hearty soups and stews, and homebaked breads and muffins. In nice weather the lodge will organize bonfire picnics with all the trimmings.

The rooms here are spartan but comfortable. The wood-paneled walls and wooden floors give the impression of staying in a small cabin in the woods. There are two baths, one for male and one for female visitors, and sinks are provided in each room. This isn't a place where you spend a lot of time in your room—except, of course, for sleeping, and nobody's ever had a problem doing that up in the cool mountain air.

Rates at the Cheat Mountain Club are $95 a person per night and include all meals and outdoor activities. For reservations call (304) 456–4627.

Tourists with an interest in the scientific must find time to visit an impressive and somewhat eerie facility in eastern Pocahontas County, about forty minutes south of Cheat Mountain Club in the town of Green Bank. The thirty-six-year-old ***National Radio Astronomy Observatory*** was built to provide state-of-the-art communications equipment for exploring the universe. The sprawling campus looks like something from the set of the film *Contact.*

Set back deep in Deer Creek Valley, the observatory is ideally situated because the remoteness of the area and the surrounding mountains protect the sensitive receivers used on the telescopes against any human-made radio interference.

As you approach the installation on Route 28, you'll see several giant satellite dishes dotting the quiet valley, a startling site against the lush landscape. The NRAO houses a 140-foot radio telescope, the largest equatorially mounted telescope in the world. Scientists use it to discover new molecules in the spaces between the stars. "Molecules," explains one of the tour guides, "reveal the birth sites of stars."

Telescope at the National Radio Astronomy Observatory

This huge telescope is linked electronically around the world with other similar devices, helping create the sharpest images possible in radio astronomy. Also being constructed at Green Bank is the largest fully steerable radio telescope on the planet. When completed, experts claim it will be the world's premier radio telescope well into twenty-first century.

Visitors to the observatory can take weekday tours on the hour between 9:00 A.M. and 4:00 P.M. daily from mid-June through Labor Day. Weekend tours are offered at the same hours from Memorial Day weekend to mid-June and throughout September and October. Off-season group tours can be arranged upon request. For more information call the NRAO at (304) 456–2011.

All Aboooaaarrrddd! No, it's not the Chattanooga Choo Choo, but it may inspire you to sing just the same. *Cass Scenic Railroad* is a delight any month of the year, but in the fall the locomotive's 11-mile winding journey through the area's breathtaking foliage is really a treat. It's all part of the state park system, and it's the nation's only authentic and operating museum of lumber railroading.

Tourists board the train in the small railroad town of Cass, on the eastern slope of Cheat Mountain and fewer than forty-five minutes from

The South Branch of the Potomac River, which flows north through the length of the Potomac Highlands, empties into the main branch of the Potomac about 12 miles north of Romney.

Green Bank. The village, located on Route 66 at the Greenbrier River, has remained virtually unchanged since the early years of this century, when it was a company lumber town. At that time West Virginia led the nation with more than 3,000 miles of logging railroad line. The renovated state-park-operated line was the same used to haul lumber from the mountaintop to the mill in Cass.

Steam- and coal-powered locomotives haul passengers up an 11 percent grade (a 2 percent grade is considered steep on conventional railroads!) using several switchbacks, then wind through open fields to Whitaker Station, where passengers disembark long enough to enjoy lunch or a cup of coffee from a park-run snack bar. Round-trip to Whitaker is ninety minutes. A four-hour trip is offered to 4,800-foot Bald Knob, the second-highest point in the state. If you're going in the fall, be sure to have a warm sweatshirt or coat handy.

Before or after boarding, most visitors stop in at the Cass Country Store. It was once the world's largest company store but now exists as a gift shop and restaurant. It's located near the depot, along with a small wildlife museum, a Cass history museum, a Cass historical diorama, and a Main Street full of locally made crafts.

For those who really want a taste of how turn-of-the-century railroaders lived, choose overnight lodging from among several completely furnished state park cabins. These restored cottages sleep six to eight people, include private bathrooms, and come fully equipped with utensils, tableware, towels, dishcloths, and linens. Woodstoves and electric heaters provide heat. Open year-round, the cabins are rented by the day up to a maximum of two weeks.

For those who like the comforts of a bed-and-breakfast, **The Shay Inn,** formerly the park superintendent's house, has four guest rooms, country antiques, and home-style food. The inn is open year-round. For information call (304) 456–4652 or 572–3771.

Rail excursions are offered from Memorial Day through the end of October. Cottage and train reservations can be made by calling (800) CALL–WVA.

There's no better—or quicker—way to get off the beaten path in West Virginia than by jumping on a mountain bike (the nonpolluting variety) and heading into the distant backcountry of Pocahontas County.

Granted, this is not for everyone, but if you're in decent shape and lean toward the adventurous, give the good folks at the Elk River Touring Center a call. This mecca for eastern mountain bikers, located in Slatyfork off of U.S. 219 (about forty-five minutes from Cass), can outfit you for day, weekend, and weeklong guided trips through the Potomac Highlands. Elk River rents bikes and an assortment of camping gear, including tents and sleeping bags, and will arrange for your meals in the wilderness. For overnight treks you can choose to bunk down in a remote backcountry campground, isolated cabin, or cozy bed-and-breakfast. Back at the base station, Elk River also has a ten-room B&B and a restaurant with fantastic Italian and Mexican fare. If you're in pretty good shape, request a trip on the famous *Greenbrier River Trail,* one of the nation's longest and most scenic mountain biking trails. It follows the path of the abandoned Greenbrier River railroad line, with a .5 percent grade the entire trip. Along the way you'll see some incredible vistas of the river valley and the namesake river, one of the cleanest and clearest in the country. For more information call Elk River at (304) 572–3771.

Virginia and North Carolina may have the Blue Ridge Parkway, but West Virginia has the equally spectacular and much-less traveled *Highland Scenic Highway.* The 86-mile two-lane highway gives motorists a look at some of the most scenic and unusual countryside in America. The road begins north of Marlinton, off U.S. 219 (about twenty minutes south of Slatyfork), and leads you through the wilds of the *Monongahela National Forest,* which leads to an elevation of more than 4,500 feet. This is extremely remote country, and the roads aren't taking you anywhere fast—but that's the point after all. Unless you're camping, it's a good idea to make advance gas, food, and lodging arrangements in either Richwood, Webster Springs, or Marlinton.

There's much more to experience here than what you see from your car. For those who want to camp out, pitch a tent at one of three rustic campgrounds located a short drive from the highway. Summit Lake Campground is just 2 miles off State Route 39/55, and it's near a beautiful 42-acre reservoir. Tea Creek Campground is 1 mile from the parkway portion of the highway and Day Run Camp is 4 miles away; both are located along the beautiful *Williams River.* Recreational vehicles are allowed, but no hookups are available. Backcountry camping also is available in selected sites along the Williams River.

More than 150 miles of nearby trails lead hikers, backpackers, mountain bikers, horseback riders, and even cross-country skiers through such memorable natural attractions as *Falls of Hills Creek,* one of the state's prettiest cascading waterfalls.

Potomac Highlands Trivia

Pendleton County claims more than 240 noncommercial caves, most of which are located on private land.

Three rivers in the area—the **Cherry, Cranberry,** and **Williams**—provide some of the best trout fishing in the nation. The West Virginia Division of Natural Resources stocks these waters year-round with rainbow, brown, and golden trout. Native brook trout are also abundant in these cold and clear waters.

Back on the road, the Highland Scenic Highway will wind you along the eastern boundary of the 35,864-acre **Cranberry Wilderness,** a protected natural area of cranberry bogs, rare orchids, ferns, lillies, and numerous wildflower species. Stop in at the Cranberry Mountain Visitor Center, located at the junction of Route 150 and Route 55, and get oriented on the area before going out and discovering the bogs, which a forest ranger will tell you is an acidic wetland typically found much farther north in Canada and the northern United States.

Also at the visitor center is a ½-mile barrier-free boardwalk designed to give tourists a closer look at this fragile area. Guided tours of the bogs are conducted at 2:00 P.M. on Saturday and Sunday throughout the summer months or can be specially arranged by contacting the Cranberry Mountain Visitor Center at (304) 636–1800. The same number will provide you with information on all the above camping and natural areas.

Driving through the Highland Scenic Highway, or any part of West Virginia for that matter, brings you up close to an amazing variety of hardwood trees, still one of the state's most lucrative natural resources. The rugged lifestyle and athletic prowess of the lumberjacks—those responsible for harvesting this resource—are brought to life every spring at the **Webster County Woodchopping Festival** in Webster Springs. The backbreaking competition, featuring woodsmen from around the world, is held here the last two weeks of May.

For the past several years, the finals of the competition have been televised on ESPN. It's a fascinating event that corresponds with the heavy spring plant and flower bloom in the mountains. Located on the banks of the Elk River, a natural attraction in itself, Webster Springs is a good ninety-minute drive from Marlinton and the entrance of the Highland Scenic Highway. For more information on the festival, contact the Potomac Highland Convention and Visitors Bureau at (304) 636–8400.

Lumberjacks and literary folk have always lived side by side in West Virginia. In Hillsboro, 8 miles south of Marlinton, travelers and literary enthusiasts can tour the restored home of one of America's greatest novelists, Pearl S. Buck. Buck, you might remember, won the Pulitzer

THE POTOMAC HIGHLANDS

Prize for literature in 1932 for *The Good Earth.* Six years later she was awarded the Nobel Prize for literature for her lifetime achievements. The Pocahontas County native is the only American woman to ever receive both awards. In 1983, the Pearl S. Buck U.S. postal stamp was first issued at Hillsboro as a tribute to its most famous daughter.

The ***Pearl S. Buck Homestead*** was built by Buck's mother's family—the Stultings—who emigrated from Holland in 1847. Buck (her married name) was born here in 1892 as Pearl Comfort Sydenstricker. Her father's birthplace, the Sydenstricker House, was originally built in neighboring Greenbrier County but was dismantled and reconstructed on the museum grounds to serve as a cultural center.

The house and outbuildings sit on sixteen lovely acres. Tours include glimpses of original furniture and Buck memorabilia. The house and grounds are open 9:00 A.M. to 5:00 P.M. daily except for Thanksgiving, Christmas, and New Year's Day. Lunch also is available with advance notice. Call (304) 653–4430 for information.

About an hour south of Hillsboro is perhaps the most on-the-beaten-path attraction in West Virginia—the luxurious Greenbrier Resort. (You know you're on the beaten path when your regular clientele has included Prince Ranier and Jacqueline Kennedy Onassis.) There are, however, some off-the-beaten-path features here, like the ***Greenbrier Bunker.*** This secret hideaway—at least it was until the *Washington Post* blew its cover a couple of years ago—is a maze of barracks and storage areas reserved for congressmen and other government officials in case of a nuclear attack. The two-story structure was designed to accomodate 1,500 people at a time. The site was selected because the Greenbrier has always been a popular vacation spot for politicians and other members of Washington officialdom. It is also far from any large population center. The outside entrance to the bunker no longer remains a well-kept secret, even though Washington is trying to distance itself from this embarrassing relic of the Cold War. Public tours of the resort are now available. Call (304) 536–1110.

The Greenbrier, of course, is famous for pampering its guests, but there's also a rugged, outdoorsy element to the place, and you'll find it by stepping into the resort's ***Kate's Mountain Outfitters***/Orvis Fly Shop. Located along the retail wing of the resort, Kate's Mountain is a fly-fisher's nirvana loaded with the ultimate in fishing paraphernalia, courtesy of Orvis, the Vermont-based tackle company. The resident spiritual advisor here is Neal Roth, one of the best fly-fishing instructors in the land. If you're new to the sport, give Roth a couple of hours with you and he'll work magic, showing you how to accomplish basic casting and trout-reading techniques. Ross also can arrange trips both on the property and throughout the Alleghany high country, which is hard to get to but where trout are easy to catch. Neal knows the backroads and trails, and he also knows how to make you catch fish. During a recent two-hour outing on the resort's Howard's Run, we landed four rainbow trout in excess of three pounds. For fishing and lesson information, call Roth and company at (304) 536–7834.

Tours galore can also be had down in historic *Lewisburg,* the Greenbrier County seat. The 200-year-old community, located about 10 miles west of White Sulphur Springs on U.S. 60, has more than seventy eighteenth- and nineteenth-century historic sites for visitors to tour, not to mention Indian and Civil War battle reenactments, dozens of antiques and specialty shops, a homes tour, and a taste of the town festival.

One of the best walking tours begins at the Lewisburg Visitor Center, downtown at 105 Church Street in the Carnegie Hall building. Yes, there is another *Carnegie Hall,* and most locals refer to the New York cultural institution as "the other one." Just like its Big Apple counterpart, Lewisburg's Carnegie Hall was funded entirely by the iconoclastic business tycoon Andrew Carnegie. Interestingly, it was the first electrically lighted public building in town and in this corner of West Virginia. Built in 1902, the ornate four-story building is the artistic nerve center of Lewisburg. It houses eleven classrooms and several art studios. The centerpiece 500-seat auditorium stages drama, musical, and performance-art productions throughout the year and is now supported by local contributions.

The building and visitor center are open year-round Monday through Saturday, 9:00 A.M. to 5:00 P.M. Sunday hours are from May through October, 1:00 P.M. to 5:00 P.M. Call (304) 645–1000.

You'll probably want to spend at least one night in Lewisburg. Try the *General Lewis Inn,* which is chock full of antique glass, china, kitchen utensils, tools, and firearms. The inn has twenty-six guest rooms, each furnished with a bed more than 100 years old. Call 645–2600 for reservations.

Five miles down U.S. 219 from Lewisburg is the quiet town of Ronceverte (French for "Greenbrier") and its provocative *Organ Cave.* Pioneers discovered the cave in 1704 and used it for shelter. However, when Thomas Jefferson visited the site 1791, it was reported that he found the bones of a dinosaur, a clue indicating the age of the cave.

Spinning Your Reels

I had just landed what I considered a journalistic coup—at least for outdoor writers. I convinced my publisher that that our magazine desperately needed a feature story on upscale, world-class fly-fishing. I also reasoned that this task was not possible without me personally spending five days on the famous Mirimichi River in central New Brunswick, the gorgeous Canadian Maritime Province, widely regarded as one of the finest Atlantic salmon fisheries in North America. Americans aren't even allowed on the river without a Canadian guide and a fly rod—no pedestrian spinning reels here!

Naturally, I was ecstatic about my impending trip, but I was also a little troubled. I had no idea how to fly fish, and I had to learn fast. What to do? Call the good folks at the Orvis School at West Virginia's posh Greenbrier Resort. This way I figured I would get two awesome trips in one. A master plan for sure! Amazingly my publisher fell for it all—hook, line, and sinker.

Neal Roth, who oversees the Orvis operation at the Greenbrier, promised that I'd be able to hold my own with our Canadian brethren after just one afternoon in his fine care. Neal's a good guy and an extraordinary fly fisher. He's one of those lanky, sturdy West Virginians who looks as though he jumped off the set of A River Runs Through It. He can read a river and handle a flyrod as though they were natural extensions of his eyes and hands. Neal's also immensely patient as he goes through the litany of leaders, tippets, dry flies, wet flies, nymphs, forward casts, rolling casts and dozens of other terms from the fly-fishing vernacular.

Within an hour, I'm casting 30 feet of line and by ninety-minutes, Neal's got me working nearly 40 feet. "You shouldn't have to cast any farther than that up there," he claimed. "Casting's not going to be your problem anyhow; it's gonna be holdin' on to one of those hog salmon that's gonna getcha."

Neal wanted to spend at least one hour of my three-hour lesson actually fishing the resort's stocked trout stream, Howards Run. Neal tied on an enticing fly and instructed me to cast over to a greenish pool that sat in front of a shadow created by a pedestrian footbridge. My first cast looped in a pathetic figure-eight line of slack. Neal begged me to wait until all the slack went out of my backcast before launching forward again. I somehow hit the mark on the next try and within thirty seconds a three-pound rainbow trout engulfed my fly and slapped at the water's surface.

"Easy, easy," coached my teacher. "This isn't a Potomac River bass!" I withdrew my thrusts and began to finesse the trout back to shore and into the safety of Neal's net.

I may have been a quick learner under Neal's tutelage, but one lesson I failed to learn was patience. After four days of salmon-less fishing on the Mirimichi, I was ready to head back to the Mountain State. Next time, I'll suggest that first-time fly fishers head up to the Mirimichi to learn the basics before stepping into the wilds of West Virginia with Neal and his trout.

During the Civil War, Organ Cave sheltered soldiers, and at one point it served as a chapel for a thousand of General Robert E. Lee's beleaguered Confederate troops. The cave provided them with much more than solace. Water collected inside the cave was laden with potassium nitrate, which, when evaporated, produced saltpeter, a main ingredient of gunpowder. The cave became a major Confederate saltpeter supply source, and today nearly forty of the original fifty-two wooden saltpeter hoppers are preserved here.

Visitors to the cave, named for its "rock organ" formation resembling the pipes of a church organ, will discover there are more than 40 miles of mapped passageways. A one-hour guided tour will take you along a well-lighted path past calcite formations millions of years old.

Tours are available year-round. From November 15 through March 14, hours are 9:00 A.M. to 5:00 P.M.; the rest of the year, 9:00 A.M. to 7:00 P.M. Be sure and bring a jacket; underground temperatures remain a constant fifty-five degrees. Admission is $6.00 for adults and $3.00 for children. For information call (304) 647–5551.

PLACES TO STAY IN THE POTOMAC HIGHLANDS

ROMNEY
Hampshire House Bed and Breakfast Country Inn, 165 North Grafton Street; (304) 822–7171

MOOREFIELD
McMechen House Inn, State Route 28 in the Moorefield Historic District; 800–2–WVA–Inn

DAVIS
Canaan Valley Resort State Park and Conference Center, State Route 32; (304) 866–4121

Blackwater Falls State Park, State Route 32; (304) 259–5216

Deerfield Village Resort, State Route 32; (800) 342–3217

ELKINS
Days Inn, 1200 Harrison Avenue; (304) 637–4667

Graceland Inn and Conference Center, on the campus of Davis & Elkins College; (800) 624–3157

Elkins Motor Lodge, Harrison Avenue; (304) 636–1400

SENECA ROCKS/SMOKE HOLE
North Fork Mountain Inn, 14 miles south of Petersburg in the Smoke Hole Gorge, Smoke Hole Road; (304) 257–1108

PLACES TO EAT IN THE POTOMAC HIGHLANDS (ALL AREA CODES 304)

LEWISBURG
The General Lewis Inn and Restaurant, 301 East Washington Street; 645–2600

Fort Savannah Inn, I–64 Lewisburg Exit Downtown; 645–3055

ROMNEY
Stray Cat Cafe (Mexican), U.S. Route 50 (1 mile east of town); 822–8226

SPRINGFIELD
The Cottage (Light Lunches), State Route 28; 822–7627

SENECA ROCKS

The Front Porch restaurant, junction of State Routes 28, 55, and 33; 567–2555

Yokum's Vacationland, State Route 28 at foot of Seneca Rocks; 567–2351

SMOKE HOLE

North Fork Mountain Inn, Smoke Hole Road; 257–1108

ELKINS

Graceland Inn and Conference Center, 100 Campus Drive; 637–1800

CANAAN VALLEY

The Golden Anchor & Port Side Pub, State Route 32; 866–2722

Deerfield Village Restaurant, State Route 32 and Cortland Lane; 866–4698

Dominic's Pizza, State Route 32; 866–3354

Big John's Family Fixin's, State Route 32; 866–4418

DAVIS

Italian Supper Club, State Route 32 between Davis and Thomas; 463–4291

SNOWSHOE

Snowshoe Mountain Resort, junction State Route 66 and U.S. Route 219; 572–1000

WHITE SULPUR SPRINGS

The Greenbrier Resort, State Route 92; 536–1110

FOR MORE INFORMATION:

Potomac Highlands Travel Council; 636–8400

Southern West Virginia

Southern West Virginia is the largest region in the state in size and probably the most diverse in terms of what you'll find there. It encompasses basically everything south of U.S. 60 and includes the greater Charleston area.

It's a land of extremes. For instance, here you'll find the state's premier recreational waterway, the beyond-scenic New River Gorge National River, as well as creeks and streams decimated by runoff from intensive coal mining. Southern West Virginia is home to the millionaires of Bramwell and Charleston, but it's also a land of great poverty—some of the worst in the nation. In short, it's a region of both haunting beauty and neglect, and quite frankly that's part of what makes it such an interesting place to visit.

Mountaineers

The rugged mountains of Southern West Virginia have long been home to independent-minded people and adventurers, including the likes of "Devil" Anse Hatfield and Chuck Yeager. The area has also produced some rugged individualists from the sporting world. Lew Burdette, the Milwaukee Braves' pitcher, won three games in the 1957 World Series against the New York Yankees. The Kanawha County native also pitched a no-hitter in 1960 against the Phillies.

Another Kanawha County native, Jerry West, made a huge imprint on the game of professional basketball during his tenure as a perennial NBA All-Star player with the Los Angeles Lakers in the 1960s and early 1970s. West is now the general manager of the Lakers organization and is still one of the most widely respected individuals associated with the game.

The pastoral valleys and hills of Greenbrier County produced one of the greatest golfers ever in "Slammin' Sammy" Snead. The U. S. Open, Masters, and Ryder Cup winner was, up until recent years, a regular golfer and resident pro at the Greenbrier Resort in White Sulphur Springs and at the Homestead Resort in Bath County, Virginia

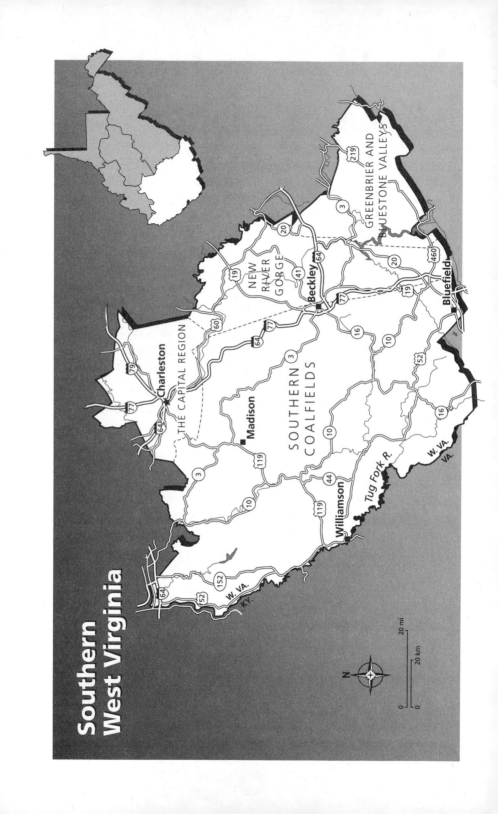

Take your time to discover the back roads and engage in conversations with friendly, colorful residents at various country stores and sites along the way. This is a fascinating corner of America, a place you won't soon forget.

The Greenbrier and Bluestone Valleys

This scenic stretch in southeastern West Virginia runs roughly from Pence Springs in the north to the Bluestone River Gorge in the south and contains virtually all of Summers County. It's a region of verdant rolling farmland, inviting old inns, and remote getaways.

Only in West Virginia can you find a bed-and-breakfast that was once a women's penitentiary. Actually, that's not quite fair because the historic **Pence Springs Hotel** was a thriving resort long before it was used as a prison. Located in the quiet town of Pence Springs, about 18 miles southwest of Ronceverte, the inn was first opened in 1918 by Andrew Pence, an entrepreneur who sought to capitalize on the idyllic location and famed spring waters of the region. (The village's water took the silver medal at the 1904 World's Fair.)

BEST ANNUAL EVENTS IN SOUTHERN WEST VIRGINIA (ALL AREA CODES 304)
Vandalia Gathering, Charleston; late May; 558–0220
Sternwheel Regatta, Charleston; late August through early September; 348–6419
Appalachian String Band Music Festival, Clifftop; late July through early August; 558–0220
State Fair of West Virginia, Lewisburg/Ronceverte; second week of August; 645–1090
Hinton Railroad Days, Hinton, mid-October; 453–1641
New River Gorge Bridge Day, Fayetteville; mid-October; 574–3834
Historic Bramwell's Christmas Tour of Homes, Bramwell; mid-December; 248–7252

By 1926 the spacious sixty-room Georgian mansion was considered the grandest and most expensive hotel in the state, commanding an unheard of daily rate of $6.00, which included all meals. During its heyday, fourteen trains stopped here daily, bringing in folks from as far away as Washington, D.C.; Baltimore; and New York. The day after the stock market crashed in 1929, however, the inn closed its doors, only to be reopened briefly as a girl's school, a dude ranch, and then finally as a state-run women's prison from 1947 to 1977.

Renovated in the early eighties by native son Ashby Berkley, the inn is once again bustling with activity and has earned a place on the National Register of Historic Places. Inside, a large sunroom and an elegant great room invite leisurely conversation with other travelers. Downstairs is the Cider Press Lounge, whose back bar was used as a

Pence Springs Hotel

set in the filming of *Matewan,* John Sayles's award-winning movie, which chronicled one of Southern West Virginia's bloodiest mining wars. Pence Springs's twenty-six guest rooms are simply furnished but comfortable. The now-covered openings on the bedroom doors are holdovers from prison days—guards once used these to look in on inmates.

Rooms for two with a full breakfast start at about $70. Dinner is available Monday through Saturday from 5:00 P.M. to 8:00 P.M. A Sunday country brunch buffet is served from 11:00 A.M. to 2:00 P.M. Berkley is a graduate of the prestigious Culinary Institute of America, and the cuisine here (trout, salmon, peanut-and-chicken casserole, to name just a few of the offerings) is outstanding. The hotel is closed January through March. Call (304) 445–2606 or (800) 826–1829 for reservations and more information.

Mr. Berkley's domain doesn't stop at the hotel. A mile down the river road sits his equally charming **Riverside Inn**, a restored nineteenth-century log cabin (built by a West Virginia governor) overlooking the lazy Greenbrier River. Servers decked out in authentic English tavern costumes present six-course gourmet dinners on oak-trestle tables with pewter service. Specialties include colonial country dishes such as fruit-duckling and meat pies. The fresh trout and seafood dishes are among the best you'll find in the Alleghenies. If you're traveling during the warmer months, get there early and request a table out on the screened-in porch. Dining semi-alfresco in the West Virginia hills makes for a memorable experience. Dress casually and prepare to spend ninety minutes wading through the courses.

The restaurant is open Wednesday through Saturday, 5:00 P.M. to 9:00 P.M., Memorial Day through October 31. From April 15 to May 30 and during the months of November and December, the inn is open only on Fridays and Saturdays, 5:00 P.M. to 9:00 P.M. It's closed January through March. Prices range from $15 to $40 (children $10). Reservations are recommended. Call (304) 445–7469 or (800) 826–1829.

SOUTHERN WEST VIRGINIA

Southern West Virginia Trivia

Charleston's Craik-Patton House, a 164-year-old Greek Revival home, was once owned by Colonel George S. Patton, grand-father of General Patton of World War II fame.

There's an almost primeval quality to the smoky ravines and deep hollows of Southern West Virginia. It's easy to sense that this was a land of spartan pioneers and rugged Native Americans, and nowhere is that feeling more acute than at nearby **Graham House.** It's an impressive log home dating back to 1770, built for the express purpose of guarding Colonel Graham's family from the local Shawnee Indians, who quite un-derstandably weren't too terribly keen on European encroachment into their region. In 1777 Colonel Graham's estate was raided, resulting in the death of his ten-year-old son and the capture of his young daughter. For eight years the determined colonel searched for the girl, finally res-cuing her more than 100 miles away in what is now Maysville, Ken-tucky. Today the two-story house, considered extravagant for the times with its thick reinforced log walls and beams, is a National Historic Site. You'll see firsthand that living on the frontier of eighteenth-century West Virginia was an egalitarian experience. Not even the wealthy, such as Graham, were immune from the hardships of isolated life.

The house is located just south of Pence Springs along the river road. It's open weekends, Memorial Day through Labor Day, from 11:00 A.M. to 5:00 P.M. Saturdays, and 1:00 P.M. to 5:00 P.M. Sundays. Admission is $1.00 for adults and 50 cents for children. For more information call (304) 466–4362 or 466–3321.

"Well, John Henry was a steel drivin' maaaan, oh yeah." This famous line, popularized by Johnny Cash, is from the "The Ballad of John Henry," a song immortalizing West Virginia's and perhaps the nation's most famous railroad worker. In Talcott, a tiny village snuggled be-tween the hills and the Greenbrier River south of Pence Springs, the leg-end of John Henry lives on at a small park commemorating the man and the myth.

According to both mountain storytellers and researchers, John Henry was an amiable, massively built black man who could work a steel ham-mer like no one else. He was employed by the Chesapeake & Ohio Rail-road, a company charged with clearing a tunnel through the concretelike red-clay shale of Big Bend Mountain. It was perilous work, to say the least. About 20 percent of the laborers lost their lives here, falling victim to all-too-frequent cave-ins. One morning, one of the foremen bet John Henry $100, a huge sum of money in the early 1870s, that he couldn't beat a mechanized drill through one of the last stretches of the tunnel. Henry took the bet, grabbed his hammer, and won handily. As we all know, however, the extraordinary feat killed him soon after the race. (Most historians agree Henry's death was related to exhaustion, although some claim he died later in a cave-in.) In any event, Henry's hammer, bearing the initials J. H., was later found in the tunnel when a concrete floor was poured in 1932.

John Henry Park, containing the hammer and a statue of the famous railroad man, was built in 1973 and funded partly by a donation from Johnny Cash. The statue sits atop Big Bend Tunnel just off Route 3. The park is open year-round, dawn to dusk.

Deep in the heart of Southern West Virginia's Summers County lies the little riverside community of *Hinton,* a picturesque railroad town that has escaped many of the urban trappings of the later twentieth century. The railroad arrived here in 1871, finding it the only practical route through the treacherous New River Gorge. The railroad brought prosperity and economic development. Today Hinton's beautifully restored courthouse, freight depot, 1890s passenger station, two opera houses, hotels, stores, warehouses, and gorgeous American Gothic, classical, and Greek Revival churches have been preserved as a living museum. Even the original brick streets and gaslights have been saved from modernization.

The *Hinton Railroad Museum,* conveniently located in the same building as the Summers County Visitors Center (206 Temple Street), explains the railroad history of Hinton through vintage black-and-white photographs, recordings, documents, and train fixtures. Be sure to look for the old C & O Railroad baseball uniform worn by town resident Robert O. Murrell back in 1897. Murrell's team, perhaps the best company baseball club in the United States at the time, actually took on the Cincinnati Reds in an exhibition game and won. The museum is open daily Memorial Day through Labor Day, 10:00 A.M. to 7:00 P.M. Call (304) 466–5420 for more information.

Interestingly enough, the house Murrell lived in is now the town's oldest standing residential structure. You can visit the *Campbell-Flannagan-Murrell House and Antique Shop,* 422 Summers Street, and get a feel for how a typical Hinton railroad family lived during the late 1800s. The wooden, three-story, Federal-style home was built in 1875; at the time, the basement level was used as a general store. Today it's used as an antiques shop, with jewelry, crafts, and home furnishings dating back to the golden years of the railroad. The house and shop are open Friday, Saturday, and Monday, 10:00 A.M. to 5:00 P.M., and Sunday, 1:00 P.M. to 4:00 P.M. Closed January through March. Call (304) 466–0294 for more information.

SOUTHERN WEST VIRGINIA

If you've toured the city and are ready for some outdoor adventuring, you've found the right spot. As you head south of Hinton along Route 20, you'll pass over and through the beautiful **Pipestem Gorge.** Named for the native pipestem bush whose hollow, woody stems were used by Indian tribes to make pipes, the Pipestem is actually part of the much larger Bluestone River Gorge. The view of the 1,000-foot canyon from the main lodge of Pipestem State Park (also on Route 20 about fifteen minutes south of Hinton) is simply awesome. For a completely different perspective, head down to the base of the canyon and spend the evening at **Mountain Creek Lodge.** The remote but modern inn, also operated by the state park system, is accessible only by scenic aerial tramway. (The inaccessibility only adds to the charm.) Have the lodge set you up with a horseback riding trip through the gorge; or, if you'd rather wet a hook, the Bluestone is famous for its smallmouth bass fishing.

Communing with nature, however, isn't the only appeal. Lodge guests are but a short tram ride away from the resort's eighteen-hole championship golf course and adjoining nine-hole, parthree links. Lighted tennis courts and a swimming pool also are located within the 4,000-acre preserve. The park's **Canyon Rim Center** regularly hosts arts and crafts sales and demonstrations by local artisans. When the hunger pangs hit, the park has a nice, affordable restaurant. There's even a day-care center on the property. Remote but hardly rustic describes the experience here.

Rooms at Mountain Creek Lodge start at under $60 for two and are available from May 1 to October 31. The rest of the park is open year-round, 6:00 A.M. to 10:00 P.M. Call (304) 466–1800 for more information.

One of the area's best water attractions (at least in the warm weather months) calls for a trip to the base of Sandstone Falls with **Sandstone Falls Jetboats.** Travelers climb aboard the twelve-seat *Miss M. Rocks* at the company's dock, located directly beneath the I–64 bridge, about 10 miles north of Hinton and a good thirty-minute drive from Pipestem. The half-hour trip is captained by a licensed river pilot, who'll take you upstream on the New River through shoals and small rapids to the bottom of Sandstone Falls, probably the most spectacular waterfalls in

BEST ATTRACTIONS IN SOUTHERN WEST VIRGINIA (ALL AREA CODES 304)

Tamarack: The Best of West Virginia Crafts, Beckley; 256–6843

Outdoor Dramas at Grandview, Beckley; 256–6800

Gauley River National Recreation Area, Glen Jean; 465–0508

New River Gorge National River, Glen Jean; 465–0508

West Virginia Governor's Mansion, Charleston; 558–3809

West Virginia State Capitol Complex, Charleston; 558–3809

West Virginia State Museum, Charleston; 558–0220

Southern West Virginia. The 20-foot-plus falls are unique because they span the entire width of the river. The jetboat trip affords an unforgettable up close vantage point. Don't forget your camera. The adult rate is $13. Children fifteen and under board for free as long as they are accompanied by a paying guest. Sandstone Jetboats is open daily Memorial Day through Labor Day (except Wednesday), 10:00 A.M. to 6:00 P.M. For more information call (304) 469–2525.

New River Gorge

Sometimes there's no overstating the obvious—this is a gorgeous place. The natural beauty coupled with the human-made makes for a not-to-be-missed West Virginia experience.

The natural drama of Sandstone Falls seems an appropriate primer to this region, considered by many outdoor enthusiasts to be among the most scenic natural areas east of the Mississippi.

The *New River* is ancient—it's been flowing on its present course for at least sixty-five million years, making it second only to the Nile as the oldest river in the world. Glaciers in the ice age buried it and diverted much of the water flow into two other rivers, the Ohio and the Kanawha. Another indication of its age: The New River flows across the Appalachian Plateau, not around it or from it as do most other rivers in the East. The New River existed before the Appalachians did, and these are the world's oldest mountains.

The river was virtually inaccessible along its entire length until 1873, when the railroad opened up the isolated region. The railroad followed the river and made possible the shipment of coal to the outside world. Today more than 50 miles of the New River (between Fayetteville to the north and Hinton to the south) and 40 miles of its tributaries are preserved and protected under the National Park Service as a wild and scenic watershed.

The best place to get acquainted with the gorge is at the *Canyon Rim Visitor Center* on U.S. 19, about a mile north of Fayetteville. The center's overlook offers the most impressive views of the gorge and the awe-inspiring *New River Gorge Bridge,* which is actually part of U.S. 19. This is the world's longest single steel arch bridge with a central span of 1,700 feet and a total length of 3,030 feet. It rises 876 feet above the riverbed. A number of television commercials and print advertisements have been shot here. In mid-October the locals celebrate *New River Bridge Day,* and it's worth attending if for no other reason than to watch the bungee jumpers, who somehow muster the nerve to throw themselves into the heart of the rocky abyss.

Outdoor recreation is plentiful here, to say the least. **White-water rafting** is among the popular sports on the river. Beginning just north of the village of Thurmond, the water churns and tosses as it begins its 750-foot descent along the 50 miles from Bluestone Dam to Gauley Bridge. (By way of comparison, the mighty Mississippi falls just over 1,400 feet on its 2,300-mile journey from northern Minnesota to the Gulf of Mexico.) The New boasts some of the best white-water conditions in the United States and is certainly among the top three rivers in the East for rafting. (The neighboring Gauley River and Tennessee's Ocoee River are in the same league.)

If you decide to take the plunge, more than twenty-five rafting companies, all certified and well trained, are eager for your business. Trips

Just Dropped In

Sometimes good luck just falls from the sky—at least in the Mountain State.

It's "Whitewater Wednesday," a major media event in Southern West Virginia. Scores of journalists, photo journalists, publishers, and TV news personalities descend on the New River Gorge for an afternoon of white-water rafting, compliments of Fayette County's aggressive and innovative tourism office.

I drove in from Washington, D.C., the night before and camped in Babcock State Park before rising Wednesday morning in a frantic search for my rafting company. The drive from Babcock over to the New River took longer than expected and, as luck would have it, Mother Nature was calling!

To my dismay, the river outfitter shop wasn't open yet, so I scooted over to the also-deserted Canyon Rim Visitors Center at the New River Bridge. Rushing to the bathroom, my heart sank when I discovered it too was closed. As I headed back up the hill toward the car, I heard a strange noise descending from the thin fog layer above the gorge. A helicopter was landing in the parking lot of the visitors center!

I noticed the helicopter had the official state seal of West Virginia embazened on its side, and to my amazement out popped then-Governor Gaston Caperton, bathroom key in hand. The good guv was even more frenzied than I as he rushed to unlock the bathroom door. "C'mon in," he shouted over his shoulder. It was an offer I couldn't refuse.

After it was all said and done, I introduced myself and thanked the governor for kindly droppin' in. "Anytime," he said. Before I could reach my car, the governor's chopper was back up in the sky, off to more pressing matters. Or, on second thought, maybe not.

run the gamut from gentle, mostly flatwater affairs to gut-wrenching, heart-stopping rapids running. Length and degree of difficulty are

The Meatgrinder

*I*nspired by my impromptu meeting with the governor (see "Just Dropped In"), I was ready to tackle the famed white-water of the Lower New River. Or so I thought.

I should preface this by noting that prior to "Whitewater Wednesday," I had never been rafting before. (No, the log ride at Six Flags Over Texas didn't count.) The young athletic guides from my outfitters for the day assured me there was nothing to it. "Just relax and do what we say. This is safer than golf."

Sounded fair enough. A piece of cake, right?

Not exactly. The Lower New was swollen from heavy June rains. Class II rapids morphed into Class IIIs. Class IIIs became Class IVs, and Class Vs. You don't want to go higher than Class V, and you certainly don't want anything to do with a Class VI. By the way, there's no such thing as a Class VII—that would put you at the Pearly Gates with St. Peter.

The first two hours of the trip were only mildly terrifying. We rolled, bounced, rocked, splashed and gargled through a half-dozen foaming Class III and IV rapids before settling in for a riverside lunch. Our guides, sensing complacency among the crew, ordered us to finish lunch and prepare for the "real" ride. We were about to embark on a series of Class V rapids.

The broad, rolling river had narrowed, now flowing around a thin strip of boulders wedged between 1,000-foot-high cliffs. Spectacular scenery. Terrifying anticipation. We were in the "real" gorge, and it was put-up or shut-up time. We approached the first Class V, appropriately named "The Meatgrinder," perhaps a bit too cocky. Our forced arrogance got the best of us, and halfway through the first series of waves our boat turned and launched 6 feet in the air.

I found myself performing a beautiful double back flip off the back of the raft, landing headfirst into the heart of "The Meatgrinder." Before I could surface for air, I was enveloped in a hydraulic, a rafting term for a spinning and churning undercurrent. It's basically a euphemism for death.

Fortunately, St. Peter wasn't ready for me yet; somehow I made it back to shore in one piece, which is more than I could say for the tongue of one of my fellow rafters. Poor guy bit it nearly in half.

In the end, we made it out of the gorge okay, circumventing all remaining rapids on account of our fright. My colleague's sore tongue eventually healed at a nearby Medivac hospital and our nerves gradually calmed.

I learned a valuable lesson that day: Never underestimate the power of white-water. These days, I'm strickly a flat-water man. From now on, I'll enjoy the extraordinary spectacle of the New from the safety of the shore.

Southern West Virginia Trivia

Senator Robert C. Byrd, a native of Sophia, West Virginia, is widely renowned beyond political circles as one of the finest old time mountain fiddlers in the United States.

planned around participants' age and skill levels. Several outfitters also piggyback the water experience with a combination of hiking, camping, fishing, mountain biking, horseback riding, bird-watching, river ecology, and even bed-and-breakfast trips.

One of the finest outfitters in this part of the country is *Class VI River Runners, Inc.,* offering beginner's floats on the Upper New, where you'll come across several Class I and II rapids (rapids are rated in order of difficulty from I to VI). More advanced floats can be had along the Lower New and Upper Gauley Rivers, with their world-famous (and not for the tame of heart) Class III to V-plus waves. At the halfway point on most trips, rafters can expect fantastic riverside grub prepared by Class VI's own restaurants, Smokey's Charcoal Grill and Chetty's Depot. Fare includes barbecue chicken, ribs, smoked turkey, top sirloin, fresh seafood, vegetables, and salads. It's a welcome respite during a long-day's journey.

Rafting prices vary widely—$57 and up—depending on the length and type of trip, the number of people in the group, and other factors. Trips are held from early spring through late fall. Class VI's base camp is located just north of the New River Gorge Bridge, off U.S. 19 on Ames Heights Road. (You can't miss the signs.) Call (304) 574–0704. For more information on the other rafting companies in the region, call (800) CALL–WVA.

Next to rafting, *hiking* is the second-most popular activity in the gorge. An easy but interesting 3-mile hike for novices can be had by following the *Mary Draper Ingles Trail.* This is the same path taken by Ingles and a party of fleeing settlers, who were captured by Indians in 1755 and taken to a settlement near what is now Cincinnati. The party journeyed through the gorge on their way back home to western Virginia. Along the trail you'll run into park service employees, dressed in period costumes, who will tell you Mary's story and bring to life the Appalachian frontier. Naturalists also will point out the region's diverse flora and fauna. It's a highly interactive experience, part theater and part nature hike.

Trail hikers meet at the Fayette County Chamber of Commerce Visitor Center in Oak Hill and carpool to the trailhead in Thurmond. The center is located downtown on Oyler Avenue, just off U.S. 19 and fewer than 6 miles south of Fayetteville. Budget about two and one-half hours. The trail's "Walk Through History" interpretive program is open most Sundays from Memorial Day through October. Tours start at 10:00 A.M., 11:00 A.M., 1:00 P.M., and 2:00 P.M. For reservations and information call (304) 877–5261.

History and hiking also meet in the gorge. Several once-booming but now-abandoned mining communities await the inquisitive hiker all along the river. In the ghost town of **Silo Rapids,** you'll come across remains of silica sand storage vessels, while in **Claremont** there remain vestiges of a giant coal preparation plant. In **Beury,** you can get a glimpse of a now-abandoned but once-spectacular twenty-three-room mansion owned by a local coal baron.

There aren't many towns with populations of fewer than fifty people that have such colorful and sordid pasts as does **Thurmond,** which sits in about the geographic center of the gorge. The town grew up with the railroad and coal operators that opened the gorge in the early 1900s. In fact, the C & O Railroad was about the only way into town since Thurmond had no streets—the only such town in America with that distinction. Nevertheless, it became a commercial and social hub and a prosperous shipping center during its heyday. More freight tonnage was generated here than in Cincinnati and Richmond combined.

Thurmond also cultivated quite a reputation as a rough-and-tumble outlaw town. A common joke heard during the twenties and thirties was "the only difference between Thurmond and Hell is that a river runs through Thurmond." The town also had the distinction of hosting the longest-running poker game in history. The game began in the lively Dun Glen Hotel and ended fourteen years later, but only after the hotel burned down. Thurmond's demise came with the advent of the automobile, and its population dwindled to its present tiny state. It is now one of the smallest incorporated towns in West Virginia. As you hike through, notice the small wooden homes (some still occupied) that cling precariously to the hillside. Many of these were built by coal operators as company housing. Take a quick scan of this hardscrabble village, and it's easy to understand why director John Sayles chose Thurmond as the setting for his film Matewan, about the 1920s miners' uprising in Southern West Virginia. (Interestingly, not far away in Grandview State Park, another drama about Matewan is played out each summer on an outdoor theater. It's about the Hatfield-McCoy feud. More on that when we get to Matewan, (pp. 76–78.)

Thurmond's changing, though. A multimillion-dollar restoration, including a face-lift to the railroad depot, by the National Park Service is under way. When completed in a few years, a hotel, restaurant, and

OTHER ATTRACTIONS WORTH SEEING
IN SOUTHERN WEST VIRGINIA

museum will greet tourists, many of whom will come in via the Amtrak Cardinal. Consequently, now might be the best time to visit the state's most off-the-beaten-path town—before the commercialization sets in. You can float into Thurmond by hooking up with a rafting company or drive down the dicey county road leading into the gorge from Mount Hope, 5 miles south of Oak Hill. If you elect to drive, park on the west side of the river and walk the bridge into Thurmond. Bring a camera, because you'll certainly want to document your trip to the "end of the earth."

Bluestone Museum —
Hinton

High Country Gallery—
Lewisburg

Outdoor Dramas
at Grandview—
Beckley

Science Center of
West Virginia—
Bluefield

Daniel Boone Park—
Charleston

For a bird's-eye view of the gorge and its eerie ghost towns, get in touch with colorful septuagenarian Frank Thomas, who is known as *"Five-Dollar Frank."* For five bucks Thomas or crew will take you on a fifteen-minute airplane ride over the New River Bridge, the gorge, and the surrounding area. Thomas is a legendary figure in these parts. In 1944 he single-handedly cleared a gentle hillside with an ax and saw, creating the Fayette Airport near Fayetteville. Besides the air tour business, Thomas has run the airport's *Poor Men's Flying School* for more than fifty years. He figures he's taught more than a thousand students to fly. Thomas can be reached by calling the Fayette Airport at (304) 574–1035.

Dozens of hotels, lodges, and bed-and-breakfasts are sprinkled throughout the New River area. A good bet is *Brock House* (304–872–4887), a 108-year-old, twenty-one-room mansion up in Summersville, located not far off U.S. 19. The three-story Victorian with gingerbread trim was built to provide lodging for guests when the Nicholas County Court was in session. It has since been renovated to include six guest rooms. The enticing aroma of home-baked breads and muffins drifts up the stairs each morning, and after breakfast guests head off to see such local diversions as *Carnifax Ferry Civil War Battlefield* and crystal-clear *Summersville Lake.* Carnifax Ferry, located along the Gauley River, was the site of a Northern rout of Confederate forces in 1861, a triumph that opened this part of the newly formed state of West Virginia to Federal control.

Probably the last place most people think of to go scuba diving is West Virginia, but few lakes in the United States have the extraordinary water clarity found in 2,800-acre Summersville Lake, which is actually a dammed section of the Gauley River in central Nicholas County. In some parts of the lake, underwater visibility exceeds 50 feet.

Disaster

Coal-mining disasters, unfortunately, are part of the history and psyche of Appalachia, perhaps nowhere more so than in West Virginia. In 1907, 361 miners died in an explosion in Monogah. In 1914–1915, over 400 miners died in separate incidents in Benwood, Leland, and Eccles, West Virginia. In fact, during World War I, West Virginia miners had a higher casualty rate than the American Expeditionary Force in Europe. While the dangers have subsided dramatically since the 1950s, risk still looms. In 1973, for example, a collapsed slag dam resulted in 175 deaths near Buffalo Creek.

Sarge's Dive Shop on Summersville Lake leverages this natural attribute by offering a host of dive charters and snorkel trips along the cliflike shores of the lake. If you're new to scuba diving, owners Mark and Eric Allen offer certified courses, including private instruction, and have plenty of gear for rent. In addition an underwater photography class is offered for those who want to take the scuba experience a bit further. Pontoon boat tours of the lake also are offered from here.

Sarge's is located at Long Point Marina, a mile south of Summersville off U.S. 19. Diving reservations are preferred, but walk-ins are welcome, says Mark. Call (304) 872–4048 or 872–1782 for more information.

Southern Coalfields

Seven rugged counties—Boone, Logan, McDowell, Mingo, Wyoming, Raleigh, and Mercer—represent a large share of West Virginia's coal industry. Although coal is found in other parts of the state, these counties cumulatively produce huge quantities of the stuff—as much as 60 percent the state's total output in 1997.

In 1742 German immigrant John Peter Salley discovered coal along the Coal River in what became Boone County. The next century saw the introduction of railroads and coal mining to the area. By 1900 the combined coal output of Mingo, McDowell, and adjacent Mercer County was almost more than the entire state's production just a decade earlier. McDowell and Logan Counties were producing 5 million tons each by 1914, and to date, over 4.1 billion tons have been produced in these historic coalfields.

The story of coal mining and the hard life of miners might not sound like the stuff of tourism, but West Virginia has done a good job promoting the cultural heritage of the region. And it's a heritage that's every bit as different and fascinating as the Cajuns of Louisiana and the watermen of the Chesapeake Bay.

The gateway to the coalfields is *Beckley,* located at the intersection of Interstates 77 and 64, about an hour south of Summersville. The city (population 18,000 and the region's largest) was founded and later named for General Alfred Beckley, the first Clerk of Congress during the administrations of Presidents Washington, Adams, and Jefferson. Beckley's home, **Wildwood,** a two-story log cabin on F Street, is preserved as a museum and is open year-round to visitors. Also of interest

One-ton car at the Beckley Exhibition Coal Mine

is the city's preserved uptown section, with its boutiques and restaurants situated around the town square.

The so-called city with a mine of its own is home to the **Beckley Exhibition Coal Mine,** located right off Harper Road (Route 13) in what is now part of New River Park. More than 1,500 feet of underground passages have been restored in this once-working mine, originally operated by a family-owned coal company in the late 1800s. Ride aboard a clanking "man trip" car guided through the mine for a look at how low-seam coal mining developed from its earliest manual stages to modern mechanized operation. Former miners are your guides on the trips and, as you can imagine, they provide colorful commentary. Be sure to bring a jacket—it's always fifty-eight degrees down in the catacombs.

The mine is open from the first weekend in April through November 1. Tours run from 10:00 A.M. to 5:30 P.M. Rates are $5.00 for adults, $3.00 for children. For more information call (304) 256–1747.

After you've taken the tour, stop in at the park's mining museum, then head over to the museum's restored three-room house, which was once owned by the New River Coal Company and housed a miner and his family. Also, don't miss the **Youth Museum** on the grounds, housed in four railroad cars and featuring, among other things, fascinating wood carvings depicting the legend of John Henry. An adjacent mountain homestead details the day-to-day lives of early mountaineers.

An hour south of Beckley along the West Virginia Turnpike puts you in **Bluefield,** a town that resonates with coal-mining history. Here you should make time to visit the **Eastern Regional Coal Archives,** housed

Black Miners

In West Virginia and other parts of central and southern Appalachia, European immigrants—notably Irish, Italian, and Polish—played a large role in the development of the coal fields. What's lesser known is the critical role played by African-American coal miners. Between 1880 and 1930, as the region began to industrialize, African Americans in search of jobs flowed into West Virginia and neighboring Kentucky at a rapid pace. By 1930, nearly 30 percent of West Virginia's population was African American. Since the 1950s, however, the massive mechanization of the coal fields has resulted in significantly lower populations of miners, including African Americans, who now represent less than 10 percent of the state's population.

in the Craft Memorial Library, 600 Commerce Street. Archivist Stuart McGehee has masterfully assembled a collection of coal-mining memorabilia, including company records, company store account books, correspondence, diaries, films, ledgers, maps, miners' tools, newspapers, and oral history tapes. Black-and-white photographs, some dating back to 1919, capture the pain and pride of the miners.

The center is open Monday through Friday from 9:30 A.M. to 5:00 P.M. There is no admission charge. Call (304) 325–3943 for more information.

Bluefield itself makes for an interesting afternoon of touring. The city straddles the Virginia border and is incorporated in both states. It's known as "nature's air-conditioned city" on account of the unusually cool summers. Bluefield sits at about 2,000 feet in the Alleghenies, high enough to ward off the oppressive heat common to the valleys. In fact, if the mercury rises over ninety degrees, free lemonade is served at the Chamber of Commerce, a quaint tradition made famous after it was broadcasted on national TV by NBC's amiable meteorologist Willard Scott.

Like most towns in the coalfields, Bluefield blossomed with the arrival of the railroad. The Norfolk & Western hauled the world's finest coal out of this area for more than one-hundred years, and the city has long been the industrial, financial, administrative, medical, and corporate center of the region. Its grand 1920s architecture is striking even today and is evident in a host of classic revival, neoclassical, and second-Renaissance revival buildings and homes. One of the most impressive is the elaborate West Virginia Hotel at Federal and Scott Streets. Twelve stories high, it's still the tallest building in Southern West Virginia. The hotel once boasted a huge ballroom, dances, and a Paris-trained chef who was stolen away from the nearby Greenbrier Resort. Today the building houses office space. Special guided group tours of the downtown area are available with advance notice. Call Main Street Bluefield at (304) 325–5442 for more information.

West Palm Beach, Newport, Beverly Hills, and Palm Springs: These cities are famous today for their affluence. About one hundred years

**Southern West
Virginia Trivia**

*The Tug Fork River, which
meanders along the
Kentucky–West Virginia
border, is the longest
free-flowing river in
Central Appalachia.*

ago, however, tiny *Bramwell*, West Virginia, was undeniably the richest city of its size in the United States. Located on a peninsula of the Bluestone River, about 7 miles northwest of Bluefield on U.S. 52, Bramwell (current population 650) was home to most of the major coal barons of Southern West Virginia. In the early part of the century, as many as fourteen millionaires lived within a 2-block radius. Their homes, needless to say, are spectacular. Perhaps the most opulent is the *Thomas House,* on Duhring Street. The revival Tudor-style home was built by coal operator W. H. Thomas between 1909 and 1912. Thomas actually had Italian masons brought over to do the stonework on the house and the retaining wall. It's estimated the house cost nearly $100,000 to build, an amazing sum of money at the time.

The nearby *Cooper House,* right on Main Street directly across from the downtown storefronts, is equally impressive. It was built in 1910 with orange bricks sent over from England. The compound contains an indoor swimming pool, among the first found in West Virginia.

To experience the life of an aristocratic coal family firsthand, you should try to spend at least one night at *Perry House,* now a bed-and-breakfast inn. It's located three houses up from Cooper House. The brick Victorian-style home was built in 1902 by the cashier of the Bank of Bramwell, an institution that had the highest per capita deposits in the United States at the time. (This powerful little bank helped finance the construction of the Washington, D.C., area's famous Burning Tree Country Club.)

Big comfortable rooms are de rigueur in the main house, but if you're looking for a little more privacy, there's a charming cottage around back that was built in 1898 for a coalfield doctor. It has three bedrooms, parlor, dining room, full kitchen, and washer and dryer. You can either have a light continental breakfast at the inn or walk across the street to the corner shop and dine on the ham and sausage biscuits that are free to Perry House guests. Rates start at about $55. For reservations and more information call (304) 248–8145.

Head west on U.S. 52 to get deeper into Appalachian coal country. About five minutes out of Bramwell, you'll cross into McDowell County, or as some locals call it, "The Free State of McDowell" (in reference to its stormy political history and independent nature). Almost immediately you'll notice how the mountains begin to close in on one another; the valleys narrow to small canyons and the sky disappears under heavily canopied forests. It's a claustrophobic feeling that's common to this part of the world. You start wondering how folks got into this remote country, let alone exploited it with coal operations.

In the town of Welch, in the southern end of the Tug Fork Valley, U.S. 52 will take you right by the stately **McDowell County Courthouse.** It was here in 1921, on the front steps of the building, that detectives hired by coal-company officials gunned down Matewan Chief of Police, Sid Hatfield, and fellow union activist Ed Chambers in retaliation for the deaths of two of their colleagues during the Matewan Massacre a year earlier. The courthouse killings touched off a series of events that led to the Battle of Blair Mountain in neighboring Logan County, in which 10,000 miners took up arms against coal company officials. It was the largest insurrection in the United States since the Civil War, and it was put down only after Federal troops were called in and several lives were lost. Tours of the courthouse are available. For more information call (304) 426–4239.

Even more steeped in Appalachian history is the Mingo County town of **Matewan,** site of the already mentioned Hatfield-McCoy feud (yes, it really happened) and Matewan Massacre. Like Welch, Matewan is located on the Tug Fork River; from Welch it's a twisty hour-plus drive along Route 52 (that is if there's not a coal truck in front of you).

Vestiges of the Hatfield-McCoy years surround you here. Snuggled into the hillside above Mate Street and the Norfolk and Southern Railroad is **Warm Hollow,** site of the Anderson Ferrell House, where Ellison Hatfield died in 1882 after an attack by three McCoy brothers. The violence came on election day in August 1882 just across the river in Kentucky. After the young Hatfield died, "Devil" Anse Hatfield executed the McCoys in Kentucky. The killings went on for another eight years, but the sensationalism surrounding the feud continues today. Some accounts in major eastern newspapers of the time cited death tolls in excess of 100 people. In reality, the ongoing feud resulted in twelve deaths.

A few years ago a fire swept through downtown Matewan and destroyed or damaged several historical buildings. A massive revitalization program is under way along the riverfront. New buildings are going up, older ones are getting face-lifts, green spaces have been created, and an interpretive center is being constructed. There's even talk of introducing riverboat gambling to the Tug Valley, a proposition that comes with the promise of transforming sleepy Matewan into a viable tourist center.

The **Matewan Development Center,** a community economic development group that is spearheading much of the town's revitalization, has

SOUTHERN WEST VIRGINIA

> **Southern West Virginia Trivia**
>
> *African-American educational pioneer, Booker T. Washington, is one of three West Virginians elected to the Hall of Fame for Great Americans.*

an interesting museum on Mate Street. The stories of the region's bloody past, as well as its proud coal-mining traditions, unfold here through fascinating photographs and exhibits. The museum sits in the **Hatfield Building,** built in 1911 by Mingo County politician Greenway Hatfield. Ironically, right next door is the McCoy Building, built in 1925 by—you guessed it—a member of the famous Kentucky family. The exhibition area is open daily 9:00 A.M. to 5:00 P.M., weekends 10:00 A.M. to noon. Call (304) 426–4239.

The recent rekindled interest in Matewan and its past is undoubtedly due to the award-winning film *Matewan,* a historical drama that starred James Earl Jones. The actual confrontation took place on May 19, 1920. At the time, the United Mine Workers of America was trying to organize the area's coal miners, but those who joined soon found themselves fired and evicted from their company-owned homes. When chief of police Sid Hatfield encountered coal company detectives hired to evict miners, shots were fired, resulting in the deaths of the town's mayor, seven detectives, and two miners. Sid Hatfield emerged as a hero, both before and after the tragic events a year later in McDowell County.

As you walk through Matewan, head to the **Old Matewan National Bank Building** on the northeast corner of Mate Street and a small alley leading back to the railroad tracks. The massacre began in the alley here, and bullet holes from the confrontation are still visible on the side of the former bank building. The building located next door once housed Chambers Hardware, where the first shots of the massacre were fired. Down the street at the corner of Mate and Hatfield is the Buskirk Building, whose second-floor Urias Hotel served as headquarters for the coal company detectives. The UMWA, interestingly, was headquartered almost directly across the street in the Nenni Building, adjacent to the Hatfield Building.

A couple of cemeteries in the area are worth a visit and help give a sense of closure to the Matewan experience. Just across the Tug Fork River, on the Kentucky side, is **Hatfield Cemetery,** where participants in the Matewan massacre are buried. It's located in the small hamlet of Buskirk, virtually within eyesight of Matewan.

About 15 miles northeast of Matewan lies "Devil" Anse Hatfield, the patriarch of the West Virginia Hatfield clan (who, by the way, survived the feud and died of old age). He's buried beneath the imposing Italian marble statue of his likeness in **Anderson-Hatfield Cemetery** in

It's the Law

The West Virginia State Archives in Charleston is loaded with wonderful historical facts and figures about the development of the Mountain State. The following information found in the original state constitution of 1872 paints an appropriate picture of prevailing priorities in this wilderness state.

Article VI, Section 33 of the constitution details a listing of some of the compensations awarded to members of the government: Legislators were given $4.00 a day "for their services" and 10 cents a mile to travel to and from the seat of government by shortest route.

This barely beat out the $1,000 annual salary of the Forestry, Game and Fish Warden and the $2-a-day salary given to members of the State Board of Embalmers.

It's all proof that the natural order is as important to West Virginians as the political order.

Sarah Ann, a small "coal camp" (i.e., village, in Southern West Virginia vernacular) located off of Route 44. Both cemeteries are open to the public from dawn to dusk.

Lodging is a rather scarce commodity in this corner of West Virginia, so you might want to start heading toward Charleston, the state capital and West Virginia's largest city, about two and one-half hours north. On your way up U.S. 119, you'll pass through the town of Logan and by Chief Logan State Park. During the summer months the park stages productions of **The Aracoma Story,** an outdoor play depicting the struggle of the Shawnee Indians to survive in a changing land. It's based on both historical fact and local legend and tells the story of Chief Cornstalk's daughter Aracoma and her lover Boling Baker, a British soldier captured by her father. The Chief Logan Amphitheater also houses other dramatic productions, such as *Little Orphan Annie;* the Aunt Jenny Wilson Folk Festival, a local event; and the annual Shawnee Living History Trail. For more information on the shows, call (304) 752–0253.

The Capital Region

West Virginia is graced with one of the most beautiful state capitals in the United States. **Charleston** (population 57,000) fans out along the banks of the Kanawha River, a major transport link to the Ohio Valley and the industrial Midwest. Charleston's actually a good five to six hours from the nearest major population centers of Pittsburgh and Cincinnati and as such has maintained a certain rugged "big small-town" charm. The relative remoteness of the capital city probably explains why so much of its beautiful architecture has been so well preserved.

There's lots to see and do in Charleston, starting with the **Capitol Complex,** located just off Washington Street 2 blocks up from the Kanawha River. Because the Capitol Building and Governor's Mansion are among the city's most on-the-beaten-path sites, few folks wander over to the impressive *West Virginia Cultural Center.* The contemporary building houses the 23,000-square-foot state museum, with displays tracing West Virginia's history from the great Native American migrations to the early twentieth-century timber and coal boom. Some exhibits feature state artists and special Appalachian craft and folk collections. Don't miss the craft shop adjacent to the Great Hall, with its wide assortment of mountain arts, crafts, historical books, novels, and music.

If you love authentic old-time or bluegrass music, the cultural center is the place to be every Memorial Day weekend when the *Vandalia Gathering* comes to town. In addition to two full days of music featuring West Virginia musicians—many of whom are world renowned—Vandalia is spiced with plenty of food and folklife demonstrations. If you missed the show, head back into the cultural center shop and get a copy of *The Music Never Dies: A Vandalia Sampler,* a tape of some of the festival's finest musical performances over the years.

Also found in the cultural center is a concert theater that offers a variety of performances, including *Mountain Stage,* the eclectic music program

Which Way Up

I've never been a big fan of commuter airplane flights. Air turbulence is second on my least-favorite list, behind only white-water hydraulics. I had to get to Charleston on business, however, and my only real option was to take a commuter flight from Washington Dulles International Airport. It was a memorable ninety-minute flight, to say the least. Flying over the spine of the Blue Ridge and the Shenandoah Valley, we caught updrafts, downdrafts and every other kind of draft. Across the Alleghenies, our 13-seat, propeller-driven plane rocked and rolled with even greater enthusiasm—all the way down to the capital city of the Mountain State.

Charleston has an interesting airport. How could it not? Any airport named after Chuck Yeager, the native West Virginia test pilot and inspiration behind the book and movie, The Right Stuff, could be nothing less than macho. Yeager Airport didn't disappoint. It's built on top of a mountain, which should not come as a surprise given that it's in West Virginia. But I have to admit that there is something strange about flying 500 feet over the Elk River and suddenly—without warning—touching ground! But that's exactly what happened because the runways begin (and end) at the cliffs overlooking the river.

I've even heard of stories of pilots flying low into the Elk River Valley on approach who've actually had to ascend for landing. Only in West Virginia.

produced by West Virginia Public Radio. This live, two-hour show is broadcast almost every Sunday from 3:00 to 5:00 P.M. The show regularly hosts nationally and internationally recognized musicians and features some of the best jazz, folk, blues, and new music in America. Past shows have included the likes of R.E.M., Buckwheat Zydeco, Los Lobos, Mary Chapin Carpenter, Warren Zevon, and the Cowboy Junkies, to name a few.

Tickets are available through TICKETMASTER at (800) 877–1212 or at the door. The cultural center, meanwhile, is open weekdays 9:00 A.M. to 8:00 P.M. and weekends 1:00 P.M. to 5:00 P.M. For more information on the center's services and programs, call (304) 348–2045.

From the Capitol Complex, hop a 50-cent trolley that'll take you through Charleston's *East End Historic District.* Here you'll find more than twenty historic buildings and mansions, most dating back to the 1890s, Charleston's gilded age. The grand, charming homes give way to downtown, with modern hotels, fine restaurants, a large civic center, and interesting shops.

While downtown stop in at the *Fifth Quarter* restaurant (304–345–2726), corner of Quarrier and Clendenin Streets, for mountaineer-sized prime rib, or, if your tastes lean more toward fish, head over to *General Seafood,* 213 Broad Street. The latter was and still is Charleston's oldest fresh seafood market. The restaurant, with its casual fish-house ambience, opened in 1976 and has become somewhat legendary in this landlocked state for its incredibly fresh fish and shellfish. If you're so enamored with the food that you want to take some home, no problem—they'll pack fresh fish for travel. Lunch is served Tuesday through Friday from 11:00 A.M. to 2:00 P.M.; dinner, 5:00 P.M. to 10:00 P.M. The adjoining fish market is open from 10:00 a.m. to 9:00 p.m. Call (304) 343–5671 for reservations.

If you ever thought of going to the dog track, you probably had South Florida and swaying palm trees in mind. The Sunshine State comes to the Mountain State via the *Tri-State Greyhound Park* in Cross Lanes, about 13 miles west of Charleston off of I–64. In fact Tri-State is owned by the same people who own the Hollywood Greyhound Track in Florida, and you can expect to watch some of the best dog racing in the United States right here in West Virginia. Casual seating is available in the 3,000-seat grandstand; more formal viewing is offered in the clubhouse area, which seats 1,200 and includes the rather nice First Turn Restaurant. Clubhouse patrons can also watch and bet on live simulcast horse racing from around the country. It all makes for a fun afternoon or evening.

The park has matinee races beginning at 1:30 and evening races beginning at 7:30. For more information call (304) 776–1000. For dinner reservations call (304) 776–5000.

PLACES TO STAY IN SOUTHERN WEST VIRGINIA (ALL AREA CODES 304)

BECKLEY
Comfort Inn,
1909 Harper Road;
255–2161

Sleep Inn,
1124 Airport Road;
255–4222

Holiday Inn,
1924 Harper Road;
233–1466

HINTON
Sleep Inn,
1015 Oakvale Drive;
431–2888

HINTON
Coast to Coast Motel on the New River,
junction State Routes 3 and 20;
466–2040

NEW RIVER GORGE AREA
Ramada,
I–64/I–77, exit 48;
341–6455

Days inn,
I–64/I–77, exit 44;
222–0511

GRANDVIEW
House of Grandview, 680 Old Grandview Road;
763–4381

CHARLESTON
Charleston Marriott Town Center,
200 lee Street East;
345–6500

Red Roof Inns,
I–64 at MacCorkle Avenue;
744–1500

Microtel Inn,
Exit 56 off I–64 on 2nd Avenue;
248–8879

Comfort Inn,
I–64, exit 47;
776–8070

Cutlip's Motor Inn,
1807 Bigley Avenue;
345–3500

PLACES TO EAT IN SOUTHERN WEST VIRGINIA (ALL AREA CODES 304)

DANIELS
Glade Springs Resort,
State Route 3 off I–64;
800–634–5233

MULLENS
Twin Falls Resort State Park,
State Route 16;
294–4000

FLAT TOP
Pipestem Resort State Park,
State Route 20;
466–1800

CHARLESTON
Ramada,
2nd Avenue and B Street;
744–4641

Windows on the River,
Holiday Inn,
600 Kanawha Boulevard East; 344–4092

Charleston Marriott Town Center,
200 Lee Street East;
345–6500

FOR MORE INFORMATION

Southern West Virginia Convention and Visitors Bureau; (304) 252–2244

Charleston Convention and Visitors Bureau;
800–733–5469

The Ohio River Valley

The Ohio River Valley sits at the western edge of the Mountain State, extending northward along the namesake river from Huntington to the Northern Panhandle.

The valley was the site of some of the first western expansion movements in the United States, and as such it was open to attack from both Native American Indians and British soldiers. Today this area of gentle sloping hills, small riverside towns, and prominent glass factories is gaining ground as a tourist mecca, with many visitors coming from Ohio and Kentucky to shop, fish, hunt, and spend weekends in out-of-the-way bed-and-breakfasts.

Of course, the mighty Ohio River is the defining feature here, and there is plenty to do on or near the water. But there are also numerous treasures to

Shades of West Virginia

New England's famous fall foliage has nothing on West Virginia for leaf peeping. The difference is that West Virginia's glory is a bit harder to get to—twisting and turning, up and down along two-lane mountain roads—and it's a less-crowded spectacle, for sure.

The colors in West Virginia are every bit as vibrant as their northern counterparts—brilliant shades of red, orange, gold, even purple. West Virginia color is also impressively draped against a backdrop of evergreen trees, waterfalls, and mountain rocks.

As you drive through the small towns of the Ohio Valley, you'll notice that every yard has at least one or two spectacular trees—usually flame-red, orange, or gold maple trees that make even the most modest home look awe inspiring. The skies are the bluest blue, the clouds fluffy white, and the mountains cast a smoky shadow across it all.

There aren't many sensory experiences more inspiring than spending an autumn morning catching trout in a cold, rocky stream and seeing the magnificent colors reflected in the water. Or taking in an open-air "leaf-watching" train trip, riding in the brisk air through miles of glory. The scenery is a bit more out of the way, but as they say "the journey is the destination"—and it couldn't be more true of a West Virginia autumn.

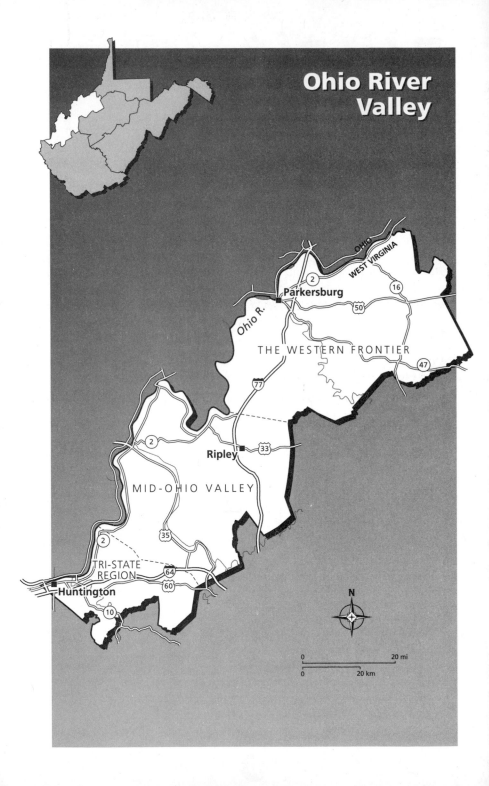

THE OHIO RIVER VALLEY

be found away from the riverbank, in the rich green folds and ravines of the Appalachian foothills.

Sharing qualities of both the Midwest and the upper South, the valley is a warm, friendly place where no one's about to get in a hurry or demand that you do, either.

Tri-State Region

The Tri-State Region begins just west of Charleston and extends westward about 60 miles to Huntington and the confluence of the Big Sandy and Ohio Rivers, the point where the states of Ohio, Kentucky, and West Virginia meet. It contains portions of Putnam, Cabell, and Wayne Counties, and it's among the most densely populated and industrialized parts of the state. Of course, comparatively speaking, what's considered densely populated in West Virginia would be thought of as largely rural in most other states.

Like most of the Ohio Valley, Tri-State is marked by low rolling hills that don't seem all that intimidating until you try driving the backroads over and around them. Most of the secondary roads here aren't going to take you anywhere particularly fast. But because they're so close to the population corridors of Charleston and Huntington, you can ramble off the beaten path without ever worrying about getting totally lost—a claim that could never be made in the more mountainous and isolated parts of the state.

Head west on I–64 from Charleston and you'll venture into the heart of West Virginia's *glass country.* The Ohio Valley is pocketed with dozens of companies that specialize in the difficult and beautiful art of glassmaking. West Virginia's prized sandstones and sands have been used over the years in a variety of ways, from extracting silica and minerals to oil and natural gas production to the making of some of the world's finest glassware.

In the quiet town of *Scott Depot,* you'll find *Hamon Glass Studio,* 102 Hamon Drive. This small shop and studio, run by Robert Hamon and his wife, Veronica, specializes in handmade paperweights, glass sculpture, and blown art glass. The Hamon's gift shop is open from 9:00 A.M.

> **Best Annual Events in the Ohio Valley (All ara codes 304)**
>
> *Dogwood Arts and Crafts Festival;*
> Huntington; late April; 696–5990
>
> *West Virginia Bass Festival;*
> Saint Mary's; mid-June; 684–2364
>
> *Mountain State Art and Craft Fair;*
> Ripley; early July; 372–7860
>
> *West Virginia Honey Festival;*
> Parkersburg; mid-September; 428–1130
>
> *Mountain State Mystery Train;*
> Huntington; October; 529–6412
>
> *West Virginia Black Walnut Festival;*
> Spencer; mid-October; 927–1780

85

to 4:00 P.M.Monday through Friday, and Saturday by special appoint-ment. Special tours and glass-making demonstrations are available by appointment. Call (304) 757–9067.

Just past Scott Depot, 1 mile off I–64, is the small community of *Hurri-cane,* so named by George Washington when, as a young surveyor, he came across a spot near the Kanawha River where all the trees were bent in the same direction. Legend had it that a hurricane, or at least a strong windstorm, must have come through just prior to Washington's arrival. The town existed as a stagecoach stop and livestock center for another century before the railroad arrived in 1873 and the community began to thrive in earnest.

West Virginia may be landlocked, but you can still catch a wave in Hur-ricane. If you're traveling with small children, start your day here at *Waves of Fun,* located off I–64 on Route 34. This water park is com-plete with a gigantic wave pool, an aqua tube, and a giant slide. If the natural white water of West Virginia's raging rivers seems too intimi-dating, try the park's equally fun—and markedly safer—white-water tube run. This is a great place to cool off and wind down in the summer months, when the lower elevations of the Ohio River Valley can turn a bit sultry to say the least. The park is open Monday through Saturday, Memorial Day through Labor Day, from 11:00 A.M. to 7:00 P.M., and Sun-day from noon to 7:00 P.M.The park closes at 6:00 P.M.during August and September. General admission is $6.00 for adults, and children ages five to eleven get in for $4.75.

After you've dried off, head for a bite to eat at *McHenry's Family Restaurant,* at I–64 and West Virginia Route 19, for some good, inex-pensive, American fare: potato skins heaped with cheese, giant ham-burgers, fresh soups, and breads. What sets this place apart from your average family-style restaurant, however, is the superb homemade lasagna, piled high and rich with fresh meats and cheeses. It comes with unlimited trips to the soup and salad bar. Best advice is to come hungry and, of course, come casual. The restaurant is just off exit 34. Call (304) 562–9177.Visa and MasterCard are accepted.

After lunch or an early dinner, head over to downtown Hurricane for some shopping. There are several interesting off-the-beaten-path shops, three of which are standouts. *Reflections of Judy,* named for its owner, who has more than twenty years experience in floral design, is housed in a two-story Victorian home on Main Street. It offers custom floral designs, collectibles, and a wide assortment of Victorian and country accessories. Judy's is open from 10:00 A.M. to 6:00 P.M.during the week (later on Thursdays), but closes at 4:00 P.M.on Saturday. It's closed all day on Sunday. Call (304) 562–1027.

Also on Main Street is **Plantation Corner,** located in the oldest house in Hurricane. Especially enticing are the regional antiques, reproductions, gifts, and home accessories. Proprietor Renee Wiles offers an interior design service, with clients who own some of the finest homes in this Victorian-tinged village. During the spring and summer, the shop's Tea Room is permeated with the aroma of fresh-baked tea cakes and special blends of tea. Plantation Corner is closed Sunday and Monday. Call (304) 562–1001 for information.

The North Bend Rail Trail, which begins just east of Parkersburg and runs nearly 61 miles west to Clarksburg, was considered an engineering marvel of its day as it guided the B&O Railroad over several bridges and through at least ten mountain tunnels.

Hurricane's Downtown Association, a group of civic boosters, operates **Hurricane Creek Heritage,** a cooperative featuring locally handmade quilts and arts and mountain crafts made of wood, glass, and ceramics. The Main Street shop also has a nice variety of West Virginia antiques, gifts, and souvenirs. The co-op is open 10:00 A.M. to 5:00 P.M. Monday through Saturday. Call (304) 562–5896 or 562–3142 for details.

Back on I–64 and heading west from Hurricane, detour into another delightful little town, **Milton.** Downtown, take a left on U.S. 60 and head to the city's most impressive attraction, the seventy-year-old **Blenko Glass Factory.** The factory was founded in 1922 by William Blenko, a British glassmaker, and today it's recognized worldwide for its exquisite handblown stained glass, some of which is found in the great museums and art galleries of the world.

The factory is run by the fourth generation of Blenkos, who beam with pride over their most notable creations, including the colorful windows found in the chapel at the United States Air Force Academy, in St. Patrick's Cathedral in New York City, in Washington Cathedral in the nation's capital, and at Riyadh Airport in Saudi Arabia. These folks are also responsible for making the beautiful, clear, rocket-shaped trophies of the Country Music Awards and were the original manufacturers of Williamsburg reproduction glassware.

The factory offers a free tour, which includes a stop at an observation deck for a how-do-they-do-that, up-close view of the craftspeople. There's also a funky and eclectic visitor's center next door, with a factory outlet on the lower level and a glass museum, military exhibit, and stained-glass showcase upstairs. The fascinating complex can consume the better part of one's day.

Handblown glass pieces
at the Blenko Glass Factory

Tours are available from 8:00 A.M. to noon and from 12:30 P.M.to 3:15 P.M.Monday through Friday, except for a week or so around July 1 and the week between Christmas and New Year's Day. The visitor's center is open from 8:00 A.M. to 4:00 P.M., Monday through Saturday, and noon to 4:00 P.M.on Sunday. Both the plant and the visitor's center close for holidays. For more information call (304) 743–9081.

Still haven't had enough? There's another glass factory in town, *Gibson Glass*, located just past Blenko in a residential area. Gibson is known for its gorgeous flower paperweights, marbles, angels, and figurines. In the observation area take a peek at the glassmakers, then stroll over to the gift shop where they sell seconds and other items. Gibson's is open Monday through Friday from 8:30 A.M. to 3:00 P.M.The gift shop is open until 4:00 P.M.Monday through Saturday. Call (304) 743–5232 for directions or information.

If you're ready for some fresh air and a picnic lunch, head over to Camp Arrowhead, just off Route 60, and take a hike on the beautiful, serene *Kanawha Trace.* The 32-mile trail (you don't have to walk the entire trail—a short stroll provides plenty of beautiful scenery) runs from Barboursville, where the Mud and Guyandotte Rivers come together, to Fraziers Bottom on the Kanawha River. The trail is open year-round. Call (304) 523–3408 for more information.

If you're spending the weekend in Milton, don't miss a visit to the *Mountaineer Opry House,* a nationally known venue for country and bluegrass music stars. Performers like Ricky Skaggs, Skeeter Davis, and others come here to play on weekend nights year-round. The cinder block theater, just off I–64, is nothing fancy to look at, but you're not here for the visuals. This is all about old-time and country music with a West Virginia twang. Grab a goodie at the concession stand (no alcohol allowed) and let the good times roll. Admission is $7.00 for adults, $6.00 for senior citizens, and $2.00 for children. Saturday shows begin at 8:00 P.M., and there are frequently special shows on Friday or Sunday. Call (304) 743–3367 for more information.

Back on I–64 and heading west toward Kentucky, plan to spend a few hours—or better yet, a few days—in the charming but often over-looked town of **Huntington,** West Virginia's second-largest city. Nestled right up against the Kentucky and Ohio borders, this historic riverside community offers a number of interesting diversions. Here you'll find **Marshall University,** whose football team, the Thunderin' Herd, is a perennial NCAA powerhouse. Huntington's also home to **Camden**

Snowed Inn

*F*or newlyweds living far from home, the Christmas holidays can pose some major logistical challenges. Which parents do you visit first? How long do you stay? Fly or drive? Or do you simply stay put? In our case, the last option was never really an option at all. Having recently moved to Washington, D.C., we were eager to get back home and visit family in the Deep South and Southwest. Like most newlyweds, however, we were strapped for cash and still a bit too proud to ask for an advance to purchase plane ticket. So, we drove. About 872 miles to Oxford, Mississippi, and another 600 miles over to Dallas.

Even on such marathon trips, Steve never much liked taking the same route twice. On the way back to Washington after a wonderful holiday visit, we decided to take the northern route, skipping most of Tennessee in favor of spurring up to Kentucky and then high-tailing through the Mountain State. It promised to be a gorgeous trip—but then Mother Nature decided to spice up our adventure with a little snowfall. Actually, it was a lot of snowfall.

By the time we hit Lexington, Kentucky, the bluegrass looked more like frozen

tundra. Unfazed, Steve was determined to make the West Virginia line by night-fall of our first full day on the road. At Winchester, Kentucky, however, he came to his senses and pulled up to the near-est hotel. No vacancies. The same story played out in Mount Sterling, More-head, Olive Hill, and Catlettsburg, Ken-tucky. No room at the inn. We had reached the end of the line in the Blue-grass State, so we crept over the Big Sandy River into Huntington, careful not to slide off the icy bridge.

The streets of downtown Huntington were deserted, and the snow drifts were building. Motel after hotel announced that, apparently, there was "no vacancy" in West Virginia. Then, as so often in the case in West Virginia, the unex-pected happened. Appearing from the winter gloom was the bright neon glow of a sign proclaiming ROOMS AVAILABLE. It was a no-thrills, Mom-and-Pop establishment—a place bypassed in even the most obscure travel guides. But the proprietors were friendly, the rate was right, and most importantly, it was warm. In a sense, the cozy place proved to be a metaphor of sorts for the Moun-tain State. We slept like babies. Snowed in and happy to be there.

Amusement Park, the only amusement park in the state, as well as the *Huntington Cubs,* a minor league baseball team; the Huntington Railroad museum; and a beautiful downtown area.

A good place to start is at the *Huntington Museum of Art,* located on a wooded hilltop near downtown. The museum was started by the benevolent Herbert L. Fitzpatrick, who donated the land on which it sits as well as his own art collection. Several other wealthy local art patrons have since given generously to the museum, including Henry and Grace Rardin Doherty, who helped fund the 300-seat *Doherty Auditorium,* home of the Huntington Chamber Orchestra.

Here, at the largest museum in the state, you'll discover room after room of eighteenth-century European and American paintings, Ohio River historical glass, contemporary art glass, Georgian silver, Oriental prayer rugs, American furniture, Appalachian folk art, and contemporary furniture. Don't miss the hands-on *Young People's Gallery* if you're traveling with small children.

Admission is $2.00 for adults and $1.00 for students and senior citizens. Wednesdays are free to everyone. Hours are 10:00 A.M. to 5:00 P.M., Tuesday through Saturday, and noon to 5:00 P.M., Sunday. Closed Mondays and most major holidays. Call (304) 529–2701.

Huntington is also home to another museum, the *Museum of Radio & Technology,* the largest of its kind in the eastern United States. It seems rather appropriate to honor such technology here since radio has long helped open up remote areas of the state with national and global information and entertainment.

Exhibits here will fascinate today's electronically sophisticated kids and teenagers. On display are hundreds of old radios from the 1920s to the 1950s, telegraph items, and early televisions and computers. A favorite stop is a re-creation of a radio station studio from the 1950s. Listen closely and you'll hear the sounds of the King himself, Elvis Presley. An adjoining gift shop features recordings of old radio programs, posters, and other early radio memorabilia reproductions. The museum is open 10:00 A.M. to 4:00 P.M. Friday and Saturday, and Sundays from 1:00 A.M. to 4:00 P.M. Admission is free, but donations are encouraged. The museum, 1640 Florence Avenue, is located very near the city's antiques district, just off I–64. For more information call (304) 525–8890.

While in Huntington, don't miss **Heritage Village,** an award-winning shopping and entertainment complex housed in downtown Huntington's former B & O Railway Station. There's much activity here, including the Heritage Station Restaurant and a renovated Pullman car. Also take note of one of the quieter attractions—the statue of city founder Collis B. Huntington, sculpted by Gutzon Borglum, the same man who created Mount Rushmore.

If you love green landscapes, river vistas, and city views, there are at least three in Huntington that you shouldn't miss. At Tenth and Veterans Memorial Boulevard (directly across from Heritage Village) is the **David Harris Riverfront Park,** deemed one of the nation's most beautiful urban greenspaces. It sits on a wide expanse of the Ohio River and is the base for several sightseeing cruise boats, a popular riverfront amphitheater (complete with a floating stage), and an annual river festival, the Tri-State Regatta, held during July. Call (304) 696–5954 for a park schedule.

A short walk away you can hitch up with **Riverfront Recreation** (304–525–5577), 201 Tenth Street, and take a starlight horse-drawn carriage tour of downtown Huntington each night. Across Heritage Village and away from the river is **Ritter Park,** a 100-acre park where it's almost mandatory to stop and smell the roses. Ritter's nationally acclaimed rose garden contains more than 1,500 bushes. The park's second must-see stop, especially if you're toting children, is the playground—and not just any playground. This one was voted "one of the ten best" children's playgrounds in America by *Child* magazine. The fairytale-like play area is cut into a hillside and features bigger-than-life stone columns, arches, and triangles to climb on and hide in.

Another great attraction isn't actually in the park, but above it. **Mountain State Balloon Company** lifts off from Ritter and takes visitors on exhilarating trips over the lush countryside. The one-hour float gives you a panoramic view of the entire city and perhaps a touchdown in any of three states, "depending on which way the wind is blowing," says operator Steven Bond. Flights are limited to two passengers, and the cost is $125 per person. Call (304) 523–7498 two weeks in advance to schedule a ride. It might be wise to book even further in advance during the beautiful autumn months.

Don't leave Huntington without taking a look at the **East End Bridge,** a mile-long steel spider web of a bridge connecting Huntington's Thirty-first Street to Procterville, Ohio's Route 7. It's the second concrete

Hot-air ballooning in the Ohio River Valley

cable-stayed bridge built in the United States and the first to use triple-strength concrete. It cost $38 million and took twenty years to plan, ten years to build. It was completed in 1985.

Just a few miles west of Huntington, off I–64, is the historic riverside community of *Ceredo.* The town was named after the Greek goddess of grain, Ceres, by its founder, Eli Thayer, an abolitionist who believed steam power could replace slave power. Like so many other towns in this part of the state, this little hamlet, built along the flat floodplain of the Ohio River, is known for its glassmakers. This is where *Pilgrim Glass Corporation* crafts its famous cranberry and cameo glass, some of the most difficult glass to make. The intricacy is readily apparent in the translucent platters carved with lattice and roses, the green and blue bud vases etched with delicate lilies on a stem, and even the contemporary opaque black glass.

The cameo glass defies description. It has to be seen to be appreciated. It's made by first applying layer upon layer of colored glass and then carving designs on the glass to create multicolored vases, jars, and eggs. There may be just two colors or as many as nine used. Red roses grace milky white glass, white dogwoods sit on cobalt blue, white daisies peek out amid green blades of grass—all in glass!

The plant's observation deck is open Monday through Friday from 9:00 A.M. to 5:00 P.M. Call (304) 453–3553 for more information. Admission is free.

Mid-Ohio Valley

The slow-paced, easygoing Mid-Ohio Valley includes the large swath of country extending north along the Ohio from Huntington up to around Parkersburg. It's a patchwork of forests, farmland, and serene river roads. It's also among the state's least traveled tourist destinations; hence, virtually everything here is off the beaten path.

A forty-five-minute drive north of Huntington, along the lazy Ohio, puts you in **Point Pleasant,** which is also the terminus of the Kanawha River. The town's **Battle Monument State Park** remembers one of the final battles of the French and Indian War, fought here on October 10, 1774. More than a thousand Virginia militiamen fought against as many Shawnee Indians, keeping them from forming an alliance with the British. The fighting allowed white settlers to push farther west into the frontier of Ohio and beyond. The two-acre park has several monuments to the brave that fell here, along with the Mansion House, the first hewn log house in the county. It was so large for its day, with two stories and real glass windows, that the settlers felt justified in giving it such a grandiose name. First used as a tavern, it now houses battle artifacts. The park is open year-round, and donations are appreciated in lieu of an admission fee. *Mansion House* is open May through October, 9:00 A.M. to 4:30 P.M., Monday through Saturday, and 1:00 P.M.to 4:30 P.M., Sundays. Call (304) 675–0869 for more information.

In 1895 the Southern Pine was in serious jeopardy. The pine bark beetle was overrunning the forests of West Virginia, devouring the protective skins of this valuable timber.

Andrew Delmar Hopkins, a self-taught research scientist from Jackson County, traveled to Germany where he found a natural predator beetle and returned with a plan and some of the beetles.

Hopkins's German predator beetles did the trick on their American cousins, and the Southern Pine avoided extinction. So successful were Hopkins's efforts to save the tree that West Virginia State University bestowed him with an honorary doctorate degree.

At your next stop you'll learn a lot about what farm life in West Virginia was like. Just to the north of Point Pleasant is the **West Virginia State Farm Museum,** with more than fifty acres of grounds and thirty-one period buildings demonstrating the hearty lifestyle of West Virginia farmers past and present. On your tour take particular note of **General,** a Belgian gelding (now stuffed) on record as the third-largest horse ever to have lived. The museum is open April through November from 10:00 A.M. to 4:00 P.M., Tuesday through Saturday, and from 1:00 P.M.to 4:00 P.M., Sunday. Admission is free. Call (304) 675–5737 for information.

Heading east on Route 2 will take travelers "round the bend" of the Ohio River—that is, to the small community of **Ravenswood.** The town received accolades from none other than George Washington when he made his living as a land surveyor. He surveyed much of the Ohio Valley and wrote about the area in his journal. That bit of history is preserved, along with many other artifacts, at **Washington's Lands Museum,** found in the upper two floors of a converted river-lock building and a restored log cabin. Land grant documents signed by Patrick Henry, a log house furnished in 1840s style, and the trappings of an old country store are the highlights here. Take the Ravenswood exit to Route 2, then follow the signs to the river bridge. The museum is riverside. Hours are 1:00 P.M. to 5:00 P.M., Sunday, Memorial Day through Labor Day (longer if weather permits); otherwise by appointment. Call (304) 372–5343.

If you're in an artsy frame of mind, head south on I–77 to the *Cedar Lakes Craft Center* in Ripley. The center stages the annual *Mountain State Arts and Crafts Fair,* a prestigious showcase for some of West Virginia's best artisans and mountain musicians held every Independence Day weekend. At the festival you're likely to find woodcarvers making ladderback chairs or mountain dulcimers (many of which are played on the spot) and specialty craftspeople churning out intricate quilts, dried-flower wreaths, sweaters, and jewelry. A big hit at one of the most recent festivals was a handmade line of ladies' accessories woven out of pine straw!

If you're passing through at another time of year, there's still plenty to see and do at Cedar Lakes. From March through mid-November, some of the country's best artisans teach others new ideas, designs, and techniques for handcrafted art. People come from all over the United States to spend a week at the center (you can stay in a dormitory or off campus), learning pottery making, woodworking, jewelry making, rag-rug weaving, quilting, watercolor printing, basket weaving, chair making, and more. The center also participates in the Elderhostel program, an international network of colleges and other institutions that offers special classes for senior citizens. More than 250 seniors participated at Cedar Lakes in 1994. For information about the center, call (304) 372–7005.

The Western Frontier

The northern Ohio Valley counties of Wood, Pleasants, Ritchie, and Wirt were once considered outposts of the western frontier, a wild and woolly region of hardscrabble farms and low, forested hills. Though the pioneers continued on much farther west, the region still retains a certain rustic charm. *Parkersburg* is the only town in the region with a population over 15,000. Nevertheless, this somewhat lonely stretch of the Ohio Valley also might be the most scenic and fascinating.

Plan to spend at least a day in Parkersburg, for this friendly community on the banks of the Ohio has much to offer. The best place to start, naturally, is the *Visitors and Convention Bureau,* downtown at 215 First

THE OHIO RIVER VALLEY

Street. Here you can pick up loads of information on local points of interest. The bureau is open Monday through Friday from 8:00 A.M. to 4:30 P.M. One interesting site is just down the street. *Point Park* is where local residents built a flood wall after a series of devastating floods. Marks on the wall show where the river crested each of the last three times; the most recent, in 1913, was 38 feet above normal.

While you're down by the flood wall, don't miss the **Little Kanawha Crafthouse,** an adorable little cottage that displays high-quality hand-made crafts from hundreds of area artisans. The selection of baskets, ceramics, quilts, furniture, and other items is amazing given the size of the shop—about the size of a bedroom. Prices range from $1.00 to several hundred. From May to October hours are 10:00 A.M. to 6:00 P.M., Monday through Saturday, and 11:00 A.M. to 6:00 P.M., Sunday. From October to April, hours are 9:00 A.M. to 5:00 P.M., Monday through Saturday. Call (304) 485–3149 for more information.

Point Park is also where visitors board the sternwheeler that takes them to *Blennerhasset Island.* The Blennerhasset story is a unique and tragic one. Wealthy Irish immigrants, Harman and Margaret Blenner-hasset, bought an island in the Ohio River, built "the most beautiful private residence in the Ohio Valley," and lived in unsurpassed splendor for several years.

Their downfall came when a prominent figure in American history, *Aaron Burr,* arrived in their lives. Burr, already notorious for killing Alexander Hamilton in a duel, had just lost the presidency to Thomas Jefferson and was very bitter. He hatched a scheme to set up his own country by seizing Spanish territory in the Southwest. He enlisted Harman Blennerhasset's help, but local officials discovered the plot and arrested the pair for treason. Though both were eventually acquitted, the Blennerhassets were ruined financially and politically after the ordeal (the mansion had already burned to the ground in an accident). They tried briefly to resurrect their lifestyle in Mississippi by running a cotton plantation, but it failed and they returned to England. Harman died there, and Margaret returned to the United States seeking financial aid from her sons. One son disappeared; she and the other son died in poverty.

Though a tragic tale, there's much to see on Blennerhasset Island, now on the National Register of Historic Places. The state reconstructed the Italian Palladian-style mansion on the original site using research and information from archeological excavations. Resembling George

Washington's Mount Vernon, the mansion has more than 7,000 square feet of space and is resplendent with oil paintings, Oriental rugs, opulent antiques, Italian sculptures, and other treasures.

Ruble's Sternwheelers (304–428–2415 or 614–423–7268) leaves the mainland from Point Park for the island every half hour between 10:00 A.M. and 5:00 P.M., May through October (weekends only in September and October). The trip on the steam-driven paddle wheeler boat, once a common site on the Ohio River, and tours of the mansion and museum cost $6.50 for adults and $4.00 for children ages six to twelve. (The company also takes visitors on other river cruises. More on that later—see pg. 97).

The boat launch is near the *Blennerhasset Museum,* Second and Julia Streets, where you can begin with a twelve-minute video about the Blennerhassets. The island itself is believed to have been inhabited as many as 11,000 years ago. So before boarding check out the glass-encased displays of ancient relics found there (don't miss the mastodon bones) as well as other exhibits unrelated to the Blennerhassets. The museum is open 9:30 A.M. to 6:00 P.M., Tuesday through Saturday, year-round. Call (800) CALL–WVA for information.

After you return from the island (or before you go), there's still lots to see and do. If you remain in a Blennerhasset frame of mind, head over to the hotel bearing the same name. The redbrick turrets and palladium windows of the *Blennerhasset Hotel* (now on the National Register of Historic Places), Fourth and Market Streets, takes visitors back to another time, when horses galloped by and gunshots sometimes rang in the rowdy Parkersburg streets. It remains the showcase today that it was when it was built in 1889 by banker Colonel William Chancellor. It was also one of the first hotels in the country to boast a bank branch in its lobby. Its elegance and sophistication made it the grandest hotel in the state, and those qualities are still evident, thanks to a renovation in the 1980s. Guest rooms are elegant and comfortable. Its restaurant, *Harman's,* serves the best food in town, including some surprisingly delicious seafood dishes. (Surprising, only in that West Virginia is landlocked.) For reservations or information call (304) 433–3131 or (800) 262–2536.

While you're still downtown, check out Parkersburg's *Oil and Gas Museum.* Not interested? Don't be so hasty. This exhibit offers a fascinating

OTHER ATTRACTIONS WORTH SEEING IN THE OHIO RIVER VALLEY

Sarvis-Fork Covered Bridge— Sandyville

Julia-Ann Square Historic District— Parkersburg

Jim Davis Handcut Crystal— Pennsboro

R. C. Marshall Hardware Company— Cairo

look at what could be a dry subject, no pun intended. Housed in a turn-of-the-century hardware store is an impressive collection of engines, pumps, tools, models, documents, maps, photos, and more. Visitors can trace the development of West Virginia's oil and gas industry, from the Indians (yes, the first Americans used oil, which was so abundant here that it rose to the surface and oozed into the river) to the time when Standard Oil arrived in the 1870s to the present day. In fact Parkersburg is still known as "the town that oil built." Outside note the enormous pieces of drilling equipment adjacent to the building. Hours are Saturday from 10:00 A.M. to 6:00 P.M., Sunday noon to 6:00 P.M., and weekdays and evenings by appointment. Call (304) 485–5446 or 428–8015 for information.

Remember Ruble's Sternwheelers, the folks who took you over to the Blennerhassets' place? Well, they've got even more to offer than the island tour. Their boats will take you on a dinner-dance cruise or, in the fall, a beautiful foliage excursion, during which you can admire the leaves as they reflect off the water. One of their most fun cruises, especially for young children and nature enthusiasts, is the **Critter Cruise,** which has those on board scanning the river for wildlife.

Now on to the more fanciful. Parkersburg's **Smoot Theater,** 5 blocks from the flood wall, is a restored movie house and the city's most popular venue for performing arts. The original, glitzy theater was built in 1926 at the height of vaudeville, and for a while it was home to some of the most colorful acts of the era. That changed when vaudeville died. It then served as a movie house for half a century—promising nurses and smelling salts for Frankenstein showings during the Depression—but eventually lost out to new competition. Today, after a renovation largely completed by local contributions and elbow grease, the theater stages jazz, ragtime, opera, bluegrass, rock performances, and, every June, the musical drama, *Eden on the River,* which reenacts the saga of the Blennerhassets. Advance reservations are required for tours. Call the visitor's bureau at (800) 752–4982 or (304) 428–1130 or the theater at (304) 422–PLAY. Prices per person range from $3.00 to $10.00, depending on tour type.

Try to arrange to spend a few extra minutes at your next stop, **Trans Allegheny Books.** This is no ordinary used/rare/new bookstore. It's on the National Register of Historic Places, thanks to millionaire philanthropist Andrew Carnegie, and its home is the *Parkersburg Carnegie Public Library,* built in 1906. The building itself is a gem: a brick, neoclassic structure with glass insets in the floor, a three-story spiral iron staircase, and behind it, a stained-glass window bearing the Carnegie coat of arms. Four floors house 45,000 volumes, as well as magazines, newspapers, postcards, sheet music, old photos, prints, hymnals, and more. The shop also specializes in book searches—finding out-of-print books for patrons. The library is open Tuesday through Saturday from 10:00 A.M. to 6:00 P.M.It's also open most Mondays, but call ahead at (304) 422–4499.

Next you'll leave behind the opulence of the Blennerhassets and take a look at how the other half lived. *Cook House,* 1301 Murdoch Street, is more than 160 years old and one of the oldest existing buildings in Wood County. It was home to Quakers who emigrated from New England southwest to the frontier. No frills existed in this tidy redbrick home—fancy moldings or any kind of ornamentation were off limits. Unusual in its design, the house is handsome nonetheless, and graceful in its simplicity. It was built by Tillinghast Cook, a jack-of-many-trades who constructed the house from bricks made on his own land. Cook descendants lived in the home until the 1950s, and a family photo album documents each generation. Don't miss the collection of handmade children's toys. The house is just off Route 50. Call (304) 485–1122 or (304) 422–6961. Tours must be arranged a day in advance. Admission is $1.00 for adults; children are admitted free.

Just north of Parkersburg on West Virginia Route 14 is *Boaz,* where gun enthusiasts will find a treat. *Mountain State Muzzle loading* has all the parts and equipment needed for building and collecting these types of weapons. The large log building also houses a collection of historic American firearms, Native American artifacts, and farm implements and tools. Call (304) 375–7842 for more information.

Continuing north on I-77 is *Williamstown,* within waving distance of the Ohio border. It was named for Pennsylvania backwoodsman Isaac Williams, who settled the area. A few miles south of town is the lovely *Henderson Hall.* Talk about curb appeal! This redbrick, Italianate villa-style manor house is jaw-dropping, so imposing as it sits on a hilltop amid gentle rolling hills looking down on the Ohio River. The three-story house has been called the most significant historic site in the Mid-Ohio Valley, and it is awesome. Today the estate, built about 1856, sits on sixty-five acres, though the Hendersons once owned more than

25,000 acres. It is the oldest standing residential home in the area, and it is still owned by Henderson descendants.

Stepping across its threshold into the giant great hall is like a step back in time. Both the structure and its contents are intact and preserved in pristine condition. All the original furnishings, right down to the parlor wallpaper, are still there. The Hendersons, aside from being very wealthy, also apparently never threw anything away. All their personal papers, from daily shopping lists to the original grant to the land signed by Patrick Henry, are still in the house—two centuries of memorabilia. Family portraits and photos add to the feeling that the original occupants aren't deceased, just merely away.

The home is open Sundays, May through October, from 1:00 P.M. to 4:00 P.M. Admission is $3.00 for adults, $1.50 for children. Call (304) 375–2129 for more information.

In Williamstown make time for another old classic, **Fenton Art Glass Factory and Museum.** This eighty-five-year-old business, run by the third generation of Fentons, uses old-time, hand glass-making techniques and modern technology to make carnival glass, hobnail, milk glass, cranberry, and Burmese glass.

A tour starts with a twenty-four-minute movie in the upstairs museum about the Fenton glass-making process and then heads downstairs for a forty-five-minute tour of the factory floor. Here you'll watch up close as craftspeople stir together sand, soda ash, and lime, plus special ingredients, depending on the color of the glass. This "batch" is put into a 2,500-degree oven until a "gatherer" collects some of the molten liquid and drops it into a mold or gives it to another craftsperson to be blown into shape. Other procedures, such as hand-decoration, also are exhibited.

After the tour, head to the gift shop and factory outlet where seconds are discounted. Tours begin every forty-five minutes from 8:30 A.M. to 2:30 P.M., Monday through Friday. Children under two are not allowed on the factory floor, but they can visit the museum, movie, and gift shop. Admission is $1.00 for adults, 50 cents for children. The factory closes on weekends, national holidays, and two weeks in July. For more information call (304) 375–7772.

Don't leave Williamstown without a visit to the **Williamstown Antique Mall,** where several dealers display beautiful collections in a two-story mall on Route 14. Lustrous glassware and tableware, stoneware, quilts, furniture, and more are a delight to both the educated and the novice collector. Hours are 10:00 A.M. to 6:00 P.M., Monday through Saturday, noon to 6:00 P.M., Sunday.

If you're craving a little outdoor activity, head north on Route 2 to *St. Marys,* where the natives claim "the livin' is easy and the fishing is great." They're probably right on both accounts. Here the deceptively named Middle Island Creek, wide and rolling, joins the Ohio River, creating one of the state's best spots for sport fishing. Trophy muskie are common in these waters, and the bass fishing is so good that the town holds an annual *St. Marys Bass Masters Tournament* each June. A few miles south the waters are just as ripe. Willow Island Locks and Dam on West Virginia Route 2 boasts largemouth bass, striped bass, white bass, northern pike, channel catfish, and a few more species that regularly bite hooks.

Running just above St. Marys down to Parkersburg is the recently created (1992) *Ohio River Islands National Wildlife Refuge,* a haven for fishermen and birdwatchers. The area's 362 acres are spread across eight islands on the Ohio. The pristine setting is home to more than 130 species of birds, including all kinds of water fowl, wading birds, peregrine falcons, and bald eagles. Rare plants and freshwater mussels (more than thirty species) are resplendent here. There are no bridges connecting the islands to the mainland; at the present time they are accessible only by private boats. For boating information contact Island Marina (304–684–3486), located on Middle Island in St. Marys.

After a busy afternoon of exploring, you'll need a place to rest up and call it a night. Problem is, there seems to be a dearth of accommodations in this part of the state, except for the chain hotel/motel variety lining the interstates and highways. If you want cozier accommodations, drive to nearby *North Bend State Park.* This family-oriented, 1,405-acre park stretches along the banks of the Hughes River and has a beautiful twenty-nine-room *lodge,* with restaurant, as well as eight deluxe cottages. The park offers the usual array of outdoor amenities, with one special surprise: a playground designed for visually impaired and physically challenged children.

Or, if you still have plenty of daylight ahead of you, head south from Harrisville on Route 16, then turn on West Virginia Route 53 and then Route 5 to *Burning Springs.* This circuitous route through the rolling countryside takes you to the banks of the Little Kanawha River and the site where Confederate soldiers burned what was in 1863 one of the three major oil fields in the world. Nestled in the green hollows of Wirt County, this spot, because of its value to Federal troops (it provided oil for machinery and illumination), was burned on the direction of General Robert E. Lee. It burned with such ferocity that the river became, as locals described, "a sheet of fire." More than 300,000 barrels were destroyed, as well as every sawmill, business, and private dwelling in Burning Springs, a city with 10,000 residents at the time.

The best place to stop and get information on the event is the **Burning Springs Bed and Breakfast,** formerly the Raider Hotel. There you'll find newspaper articles, historical information, and more on the great fire. It's also a wonderful place to stay. The original structure was built about 1840, and today it's been restored to a lovely inn with brass beds and gorgeous quilts. The B & B boasts five guest rooms, one with private bath; a large country breakfast; and beautiful views of the river and surrounding woodlands. The inn does not allow pets, children, or smoking. Rates are $55 for the private room, $45 for the semiprivate. Call (304) 275–0896 for reservations and information.

Where Deer Don't Hide

*O*ne of the most awesome sights in a state chock-full of beauty are the deer, seemingly tame, that appear everywhere—beside the roadways, near your cabin, by your car.

In West Virginia, deer are so ubiquitous that they appear to be much less like the shy, tenative animals hiding just inside the tree line and more like grazing domestic cattle.

When we first began traveling in West Virginia, we would slam on the brakes and roll down our windows, so unaccustomed we were to seeing these gentle, beautiful animals (no doubt to the great consternation of drivers behind us!). Occasionally we would be honked at, and after we muttered and glared at the perpetrator, we realized they were probably acting out of concern for the deer— the more they become accustomed to cars, the more likely they were to walk in front of one as if it's no threat.

On many occasions, while driving early in the morning or just at dusk, the deer would slowly appear out of the gloom, usually in small groups, grazing on the grass beside the road. As you passed by slowly, you could see several other groups just inside the woods. Once, while riding in the back of a pickup truck on the way back from a day spent canoeing near North Bend State Park in Ritchie County, we saw dozens and began to count them. We had reached over 100 when we stopped. On another occasion, several deer alternately grazed and walked beside a large group of us going into a mountain-top restaurant. (They were headed for the salad bar, I think!)

Still, after many trips to the mountains and seeing literally hundreds of deer, our joy at seeing them—and the other bounties of nature West Virginia offers— will never diminish.

PLACES TO STAY IN THE OHIO RIVER VALLEY
(ALL AREA CODES 304)

HUNTINGTON
Radission Hotel
Huntington, 1001 Third
Avenue; 525–1001

MILTON
The Cedar House,
I–64, exit 28; 743–5516

PARKERSBURG
Comfort Suites,
I–77 and State Route 14
South, exit 170;
489–9600

Blennerhassett Hotel,
Fourth and Market Streets;
422–3131

RIPLEY
Cedar Lakes Conference
Center, I–77 South Ripley;
372–7860

PROCTOR
Thistle Dew Farm,
State Route 89;
455–1728

PLACES TO EAT IN THE OHIO VALLEY
(ALL AREA CODES 304)

HUNTINGTON
Damon's at the Radisson,
1001 Third Avenue;
525–1001

HARRISVILLE
Pizza House,
902 East Main Street;
643–2675

WILLIAMSTOWN
da Vinci's Italian
Restaurant,
215 Highland Avenue;
375–3633

PARKERSBURG
Harman's at the
Blennerhassett,
Fourth and Market Streets;
422–3131

FOR MORE INFORMATION:

Cabell/Huntington
Convention and Visitors
Bureau;
525–7333

Parkersburg/Wood County
Visitors and Convention
Bureau; 428–1130

Central West Virginia

entral West Virginia is a gentle place of small towns, tidy farms, country roads, and rolling green woodlands. The region is dotted with communities whose names are as colorful as the people who've lived there for centuries. Hominy Falls, Tallmansville, Pickle Street, Stumptown, and Speed line the two-lane roads with little stores, a few houses, and some of the friendliest people to be found anywhere.

Central West Virginia is a sportsman's paradise. Its landscape is dominated by six lakes: Summersville Lake in the south, Sutton Lake and Burnsville Lake in the midsection, and Tygart, Stonewall Jackson, and Stonecoal Lakes in the north. The heart of the Mountain State is also a land of rivers. Here the Elk, the Williams, the Cherry, the Buckhannon, the Cranberry, and the Kanawha snake through this land, providing great fishing and canoeing opportunities.

This is a remote land but one that's sprinkled with unusual attractions and festivals. Take your time and enjoy the scenery, for the pace of life here is relaxed and good for the soul.

Bluegrass Heartland

he moniker here applies to both the predominant music and the landscape of bucolic Calhoun, Roane, and Clay Counties—agricultural areas rich in timber, pastureland, and old-time musicians.

The routes given here take a bit of pioneer spirit if you are to discover the treasures of life hidden off of the interstates. So grab a cup of coffee and a road map and give yourself some time, for there's much to see in this quiet and pretty corner of West Virginia.

After you leave Burning Springs on Route 5, jump over onto State Route 14 and head into Roane County to *Spencer,* where, in the middle of October, the locals are celebrating their black walnut harvest in grand style. They host a four-day festival complete with singing, dancing, fiddling, turkey calling, flea markets, black walnut bake offs, and the nuttiest parade you've ever seen. Nearby *Arnoldsburg,* in Calhoun County, is

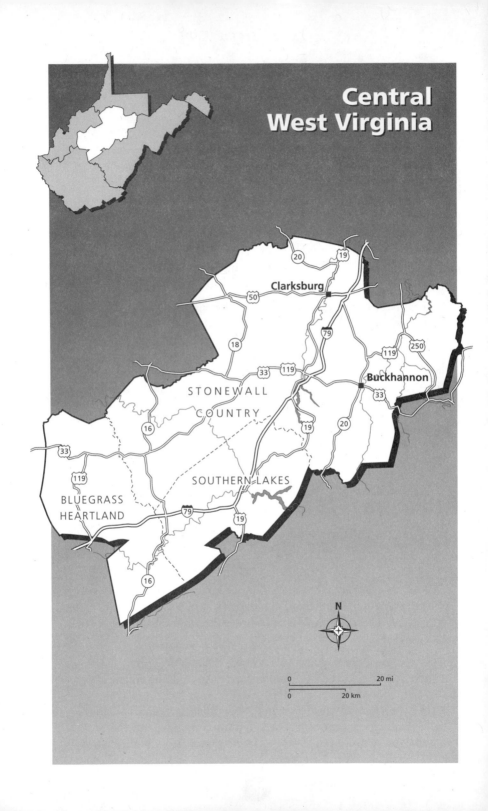

Central
West Virginia

Best Annual Events in Central West Virginia (All area codes 304)

also busy in October celebrating the *West Virginia Molasses Festival,* an event dripping with homegrown mountain music and delicious food.

In this part of the state, there are many wonderful places to shop, but don't look for any malls. Stores are tucked away—small gems just waiting for the adventurous shopper. One of them is found just south of Arnoldsburg on Route 16 in the town of *Chloe.* Here you'll uncover some of the country's finest basket weaving. Local artisans Tom and Connie McColley, for instance, have a studio where they specialize in traditional hand-split white-oak baskets. The *McColley Studio* is open by appointment only. If you're lucky the McColleys might entertain you with a demonstration of their meticulous craft. Call ahead for tours and times at (304) 655–7429.

About 26 miles south of Chloe on winding Route 16 (don't plan on setting any land-speed records in rolling Central West Virginia) is the quaint riverside town of *Clay.* This is the place to be the first weekend in September for the annual *Golden Delicious Festival* (304–587–7652). Musicians, crafters, and makers of good eats gather to celebrate the 1912 appearance of a golden delicious seedling on a Clay County farm. No one knows its origin, but folks hereabouts believe the golden delicious and its ancestors produce "the finest apple of all time." After the festival head over to the gentle Elk River, which runs right through town, and launch a canoe or wet a hook. This is one of the region's best trout fishing waters, and come early September the fall fishing should be heating up again. Also, while in Clay, be sure to stop in at the *Craft Cooperative Registry,* 99 School Street, for authentic mountain crafts made by local artists. Call (304) 587–7652.

Best Annual Events in Central West Virginia (All area codes 304)

Irish Spring Festival,
Ireland; mid–March;
452–8962

Feast of the Ramson,
Richwood; late April;
846–6790

Chili in the Hills Cookoff,
Clarksburg; early June;
842–5966

West Virginia State Folk Festival,
Glenville; late June;
462–8427

Lewis County Fair,
Jackson's Mill; late July;
269–7043

Cherry River Festival,
Richwood;
first week of August;
846–6790

Storytelling Festival,
Jackson's Mill;
mid-October; 269–7328

Southern Lakes

The Southern Lakes region contains parts of Nicholas, Webster, and Braxton Counties, an area loaded with natural scenery, sparkling though underutilized lakes, and miles of lonely but scenic country roads.

In far eastern Nicholas County, about a ninety-minute drive from the town of Clay, is **Richwood,** the gateway to the Monongahela National Forest and the Highland Scenic Highway (both of which we visited in "The Potomac Highlands"). Each April, Richwood hosts the **Feast of the Ransom,** one of the state's largest ramp festivals, and for sure an event not for the gastronomically challenged. A ramp, you may remember, is a potently flavored wild scallion, a vegetable with staying power.

License to Win

*E*arl and I were noticeably punchy. We had just spent the better part of two days driving through West Virginia, talking to tourism, industry and economic development officials for a magazine story we were researching. We still had one last travel leg ahead of us—a two and one-half-hour drive from Charleston up to Morgantown, the sight of our final interview before we headed east over the mountains and back to Washington, D.C.

Somewhere deep in Central West Virginia, between Sutton and Weston along I–79, Earl hatched another of his crazy ideas. We were going to settle an ongoing dispute over which state was superior—West Virginia or Pennsylvania. A little background is in order: Earl's a proud—maybe even too proud—alum of Penn State University. He's never been too big of a fan of West Virginia, something to do with the Mountaineer–Nittany Lion football rivalry that goes way back. Earl decided that we should take a survey of cars passing us along the highway from Sutton to Morgantown. If the bulk of cars happened to bear Pennsylvania license plates, as Earl confidently predicted, the Keystone State would win. I inquired to his logic, and Earl said something to the effect that Pennsylvanians were more mobile, more

"worldly," and more eager to get home than West Virginians. Bored, and a little irritated, I agreed to the madness and we began to tally license plates.

Through Central West Virginia, the Mountain State was clearly in the lead, 18 cars to 11. I told Earl only a touchdown could salvage his nonsense theory. Approaching Morgantown and the Pennsylvania border, the game tightened. Twenty-seven cars for West Virginia, 21 for the Keystone State. With 7 miles to go to the first exit in Morgantown and the end of the game, Earl's Nittany Lions played catch up, coming within three at 31 to 28 (although I still dispute Earl's accounting). With less than a mile to paydirt, I pulled over to the left lane and allowed a speeding BMW to pass—this would hopefully settle the score for good. The car blew by at 90 MPH and we had to crane our necks to make out the blur of a blue license plate—New Jersey!

The game ended game with a West Virginia victory—in more ways that one. Two miles up the interstate, a West Virginia Highway Patrol car had stopped the speeding New Jerseyan. "Score another win for the Mountaineers," I shouted to Earl. His only reply was "that would have never happened in Pennsylvania." Sore loser, for sure.

It grows abundantly in rocky West Virginia hills and is often the first green vegetation to sprout on the hillsides in late March and early April. In pioneer times the ramp supposedly saved many a starving soul and helped prevent scurvy. Today the hearty leeklike vegetable is a local favorite and is often fried with ham and served with beans and potatoes. The Richwood festival, sponsored by the locally based International Ramp Association, is held at the local high school, 1 Valley Way, where you're seated elbow to elbow with those who come back for more every year. Afterward don't skimp on either the Alka Seltzer or the Binaca.

From Richwood, you're also about equal distance from the attractions of nearby Summersville Lake (see "Southern West Virginia") and the high mountain country of the Cranberry Wilderness area (see "The Potomac Highlands").

After Richwood, you might also want to get off the main drag and do a little sight-seeing on county roads as you head up to **Sutton.** Take Route 55 to Muddlety, then take the county road through Enoch before catching Route 16 again near Clay. This time go north; then get on I–79 briefly to Sutton. It may sound out of the way (what isn't in this part of the state?), but the drive through the countryside is interesting and serene.

Roots of Country Music

*A*lthough Nashville claims the title, "Music City U.S.A.," the seeds of country music in America were planted far from the neon glow of Music Row. Most music scholars will tell you that country music originated in the hills and hollows of Appalachia, in places like Galax, Virginia; Jefferson, North Carolina; Monticello, Kentucky; Bristol, Tennessee; and throughout the tiny coal camps and villages of Central and Southern West Virginia.

To be exact, the roots of country music go back to seventeenth-century Ireland, and were transplanted to the New World along with the Scotch-Irish settlers who carved out a living in the Appalachian frontier a century later.

Over time, those Irish folk ballads, jigs, and reels were transformed into a distinct American mountain music, which later evolved to old-time string music, bluegrass, country-western and "honky-tonk" music. Although today's prevailing "Nashville Sound" has strayed far from its roots, real mountain music can still be heard throughout the Southern Appalachians, especially at the dozens of festivals and fairs staged in the Mountain State. In addition, countless informal gatherings are commonplace in rural West Virginia. They're not hard to find, either. Just inquire in any local music store, and you're bound to find a "pickin' parlor" or a "front-porch gathering" within a short drive.

In Sutton grab your wallet again, for here's another not-to-be-missed opportunity to own a handcrafted item or two. Head to Main Street's **Landmark Studio for the Arts,** housed in a beautiful nineteenth-century building that was once a Baptist, Presbyterian, and Methodist church. (Note the art nouveau stained-glass windows.) Knickknacks, however, are the least the studio has to offer. The studio's stage hosts the best local musicians in the state, including the West Virginia Symphony's Montani String Quartet and Melvin Wine, a Braxton County fiddler who received the National Endowment of the Humanities Heritage Fellowship, an award given to those with the finest folk traditions.

Artists from around the world exhibit their work in the studio's lobby. Here you'll find fine art and sophisticated designer crafts, such as hand-painted silk, hot-glass sculpture, and even contemporary Chinese soapstone pieces. Local resident Bill Hopen, an internationally known sculptor, often exhibits here as well. The studio is open to the public and tours can be arranged, but hours tend to vary and change frequently. Call (304) 765-5611 in advance for hours and more information.

While you're in Sutton you'll have a good opportunity to get wet. **Sutton Lake** has 1,500 surface acres of water recreation, including a marina with boat rentals. The lake is located just off I-79, and anglers come from everywhere to hook into the excellent largemouth bass, smallmouth bass, and spotted bass. Even if you don't enjoy fishing, you can take a spin around the lake in a boat, enjoying the beautiful scenery of the **Elk River Wildlife Management Area,** which abuts the lake. The park is open year-round, dawn to dusk. Call (304) 587-7652.

So glorious is this area for fishermen that some say it's where righteous anglers go when they die. You can also grab your fishing pole and splash over to nearby **Burnsville Lake.** Just north on I-79, this lake was formed when the U.S. Army Corp of Engineers dammed the Little Kanawha River. Bass, crappie, muskie, and channel catfish are abundant in these 968-acre waters. Surrounding the reservoir are 12,000 acres known as the **Burnsville Wildlife Management Area,** which at the right time of year is home to migrating water fowl, grouse, quail, turkey, deer, and innumerable bowhunters. Motel accommodations and camping are abundant, including the **Bulltown Campgrounds,** which is waterside. Operated by the Corp of Engineers, more than 200 sites are available from the first week in April to December 1. For reservations and information call (304) 452-8006.

After you've done all the fishing you can stand (or all your spouse can stand for you to do), there's a lot to see around the lake on foot. Head

BEST ATTRACTIONS IN CENTRAL WEST VIRGINIA (ALL AREA CODES 304)

Jackson's Mill and Historic District,
Weston; 269–5100

West Virginia State Wildlife Center,
French Creek; 924–6211

Little Hungary Farm Winery, Buckhannon;
472–6634

Mountain Air Balloons, Buckhannon; 472–0792

Central West Virginia Farmers Market;
Weston, 269–2667

over to the **Bulltown Historic Area,** where the U.S. Army Corp of Engineers moved several log structures to prevent their destruction when the dam was being built. Originally built between 1815 and 1870, the pioneer settlements were disassembled by the corps, moved, and then reconstructed right near the campgrounds. Today, during the warm weather months, living history demonstrations show how quilting, clothes washing, gardening, cooking, and other household chores were accomplished by nineteenth-century pioneers of the backcountry. This site was also where the *Battle of Bulltown* raged, a twelve-hour skirmish between Union and Confederate soldiers fought on October 13, 1863. The South, led by Stonewall Jackson's cousin, Colonel William L. Jackson, was attempting to capture the Union garrison stationed at Bulltown.

Also in Bulltown don't miss the early nineteenth-century *Cunningham Farmhouse,* a dogtrot-style house seized by the Union forces during the war, which bears the bullet holes to prove it. Further down the trail, which takes you along the *Weston and Gauley Bridge Turnpike*—used by both North and South to transport supplies—you'll find *Johnson House,* built in 1883 by a freedman, and *St. Michaels Church,* one of the first Catholic churches in the state. It rests on a hill, overlooking the battle site. At 11:00 A.M. every Sunday in season (see later) a tour is given that discusses the development of religion in Appalachia. During the second week of each July, in the adjacent meadow, historians reenact the Battle of Bulltown.

Also in July, Bulltown offers a special treat for kids with an interest in what school was like more than a century ago—quite an eye-opener for our technologically sophisticated children today. For three hours kids attend school in rural Appalachia of the mid-1800s, with games, lessons, and homework from authentic period texts.

An interpretive center shows a six-minute show on the lake and its facilities and houses turn-of-the-century memorabilia and Civil War battle artifacts. There's also a mystery explored here: No one knows what happened to a settlement of Native Americans, led by Captain Bull, a Delaware Indian chieftain. Follow the 1-mile interpretive trail around the grounds, or better yet, take the 2:00 P.M. tour of the houses, church, and battlefield. The center is open from May 1 to September 1, 10:00 A.M. to 6:00 P.M., but closes two hours earlier from September 1 to

October 30. It's closed from October 30 to May 1. Call (304) 452–8170 for more information.

Stonewall Country

ewis, Gilmer, Upshur, and Harrison Counties contain the largest towns in the region, most of which are close to I–79. But don't spend all your time on the interstate because most of the goodies are way off the beaten path. This route will leave your car trunk filled with arts and crafts, your head swimming in history, your stomach filled with good food, and your toes tapping a happy beat.

From Burnsville Lake veer slightly to the west on Route 5 to *Glenville,* home of the Stonewall Jackson Jubilee, an annual Labor Day event for crafters (see details, pg. 118). If you're in town in June, follow your ears to *the West Virginia State Folk Festival* (304–462–8427). Fiddles, banjos, mandolins, autoharps, and hammered dulcimers ring through the streets. If you've ever wanted to learn how to square dance, the festival is the place to be.

Now head north, either back on I–79 or on Route 33, into *Weston,* a community planned by Stonewall Jackson's grandfather. This charming little city with Victorian mansions and gingerbread-bedecked homes is famous locally as *"The Christmas Town"* because of its spectacular light show during the holidays. Beginning the day after Thanksgiving and lasting through New Year's Day, a quarter of a mile of Main Street is illuminated with blue and white snowflake lights that dance along to a choreographed computer program. A lighted Santa and his reindeer fly overhead, above all the downtown storefronts, which also have been adorned with an incredible array of lights and designs. Across the street from the courthouse, on Center Avenue, sits a 37-foot blue spruce, glowing brilliantly with hundreds of colored lights.

Interesting landmarks abound in Weston, like the *Old Weston State Hospital,* located on Second Street. This imposing structure is actually the largest handcut stone building in the United States and one of the largest in the world. Another building of note is Lewis County's only public library. It is housed in the historic *Jonathan-Louis Bennett House,* 148 Court Avenue, once home to one of Weston's most prominent families. The seventeen-room High Victorian Italianate mansion contains a few pieces of original furniture and other furnishings amid the book stacks. Visitors to the library are allowed into certain sections of the home, which offer a glimpse of life during the Victorian era. The entire house can be viewed by

Central West Virginia Trivia

Central West Virginia native son and Confederate hero, Thomas "Stonewall" Jackson, died from wounds inflicted after being accidentally shot by one of his fellow soldiers in a battle outside of Fredericksburg, Virginia.

special tour arrangements. The Louis Bennett Library is open Monday through Friday 10:00 A.M. to 6:00 P.M. and Saturday 10:00 A.M. to 2:00 P.M. Call (304) 269–5151 for more information.

While you're in town you might take a look at the *Central West Virginia Genealogical and Historical Library and Museum,* 345 Center Street. The 113-year-old brick building was once a one-room schoolhouse used to educate African-American children in the county. The school closed as a segregated institution in 1954 and up until a few years ago was used as a classroom for special education students. Today it's on the National Register of Historic Places and is run by the Hacker's Creek Pioneer Descendants. This group is dedicated to preserving the memory of the Scottish and German pioneers, whose settlements during the American Revolution served as the buffer zone between the new democracy in the East and the English and the Indians in the West.

Because it sat on the cusp of civilization at the time, no other part of the nation was as ravaged by border warfare than this stretch of West Virginia. During the 1790s many of the pioneers in the area moved farther west and became the first to settle Ohio, Indiana, and Illinois. The library and museum contains a large volume of historical documents and a genealogy archive that help trace the region's turbulent history. Admission is $1.00 for nonmembers. The library is open Tuesday, Wednesday, and Friday from 10:00 A.M. to 3:00 P.M., Monday and Thursday from 10:00 A.M. to 8:00 P.M., and Saturday from 10:00 A.M. to 2:00 P.M. Call (304) 269–7091 for information.

If you're in the mood for a picnic, Weston has a delightful *Farmers' Market* bursting with fresh, local produce; handcrafted furniture; and some very good West Virginia wines. It's located right as you come into town on Route 33 on the right. Also, a few turns off Route 33 is an unusual place to help fill up your picnic basket. *Smoke Camp Crafts* has homegrown table teas, Appalachian herbs, and a huge selection of jams and jellies made with wild and organically cultivated fruits (you can also pick up a few cleansing lotions at the same time). Traditional and exotic herb blends here run the gamut: the Headache Blend, the Herbal Moth Repellent, the High-Blood-Pressure Blend, the Hot Flash Tea, Menopause Blend Tea, and P.M.S. Capsules.

Owners Dot and Bob Montgillion are more than happy to share their insight and will even arrange for special garden tours and nature hikes.

You might want to pick up a copy of Dot Montgillion's book, *Modern Uses of Traditional Herbs,* which details the history, cultivation, preparation, and use of seventy-six herbs. Smoke Camp Crafts is located on Smoke Camp Run Road, about 5 miles northwest of Weston. Call the Montgillions at (304) 269–6416 for more information and for directions.

Lost in Grassy Lick

*O*ne of our first jaunts into Central West Virginia also became one of our most memorable. Steve was determined to fish a section of Stonewall Jackson Lake that he heard produced "monster" bass. I was mostly interested in the scenery and the beautiful spring weather.

We reserved a small boat from a local marina, about a forty-five-minute drive from our wilderness campsite. I was once again forced to stay in the wilds after my husband dismissed the infinitely more convenient lakeside campground as being "too commercial." So, when Saturday morning arrived we were forced to race like the wind in order to get to the marina and check out our boat at the assigned time. I was relying on my better-half's navigational skills, which are nowhere near as good as he wants to believe. Nevertheless, Steve assured me the little gray road on the map would lead to the lake and an enjoyable morning on the water.

We headed out confidently but soon found ourselves hopelessly lost in the middle of an endless sheep pasture. We turned and twisted over miles of tiny farm roads before finding ourselves at a disheveled, but stocked-to-the-roof country store. I would have thought it "quaint," if we hadn't been traversing green acres for the past hour.

Inside the store, we were greeted by a group of elderly gentlemen, one of whom, the proprietor, was perched behind a counter containing every possible piece of sporting equipment imaginable. The men eyed us silently, but with considerable interest.

Steve tentatively approached the fellow behind the counter, map in hand, and explained our dilemma. The proprietor scratched his head, looked over at his buddies, and shouted in the best Don Knotts-impersonation I've ever heard: "You got lost on the road to Grassy Lick? Nobody's every got lost on the road to Grassy Lick before!" A bustle of group laughter ensued. You would have thought we asked who was buried in Grant's Tomb. After more laughter, the store owner snorted, and with one grizzled finger traced our route back down to the lake.

We left humbled but ultimately had a great morning on the lake and a wonderful weekend. We still laugh about the disgusted group of old fellows who relished in our miserable navigational skills on that "bustling highway" leading to Grassy Lick. Who knows, maybe one day we'll have the pleasure of watching them roll down their windows and ask for directions on the traffic-choked arteries of Washington, D.C., or Atlanta. But then again, maybe not.

CENTRAL WEST VIRGINIA

OTHER ATTRACTIONS WORTH SEEING
IN CENTRAL WEST VIRGINIA

Anna Jarvis House —
Webster

*Clarksburg Downtown
Historical District*—
Clarksburg

*West Virginia
Artworks*—
Clarksburg

There's another herb shop just west of town on Route 33 in nearby Alum Bridge. ***La Paix Farm,*** run by the affable Myra Bonhage-Hale, produces organically grown herbs, "sophisticated produce," and crafts. The farm's original residence is a restored, 200-year-old cabin reputed to have been used as a safe house by the Underground Railroad to hide runaway slaves on their way to freedom. The front part of the house, a charming two-story Victorian, was built in 1910. *La Paix* means "peace" in French, and the setting here amid the quiet woodlands of Lewis County is certainly relaxed. Throughout the year Bonhage-Hale and fellow West Virginia artisans and naturalists sponsor various garden and herbal workshops and tours. Call (304) 269–7681.

Just off the interstate south of Weston is the rambling, cold, and clear ***Stonewall Jackson Lake.*** Its pristine waters and 82 miles of shoreline are perhaps best viewed on board the **Stonewall Jackson *paddle-wheeler,*** which takes visitors out on cruises lasting for approximately two hours. The best bets are the laid-back dinner and brunch cruises. Adult rates are $8.00 ($5.00 for children ages two to ten) for sightseeing tours, $22.00 for dinner, and $15.00 for brunch. Children under two are free. Dinner cruise departure times are 6:00 P.M. every Friday and Saturday May through September 15, and one hour earlier in April and September 15 through October. Private dinners and charters are available Monday through Thursday. Call (304) 472–3772 for more information.

There's lots to do off the water as well. The Army Corps of Engineers, which supervised the building of the dam on the West Fork River, has a visitor center with displays and artifacts about the dam's construction (in season, tours of the dam are also available). A state park visitor center, near the marina, provides information and exhibits on the area's plentiful wildlife. After a quick orientation, try a leisurely stroll along the lake's nature trails to view the legendary songbirds, hawks, eagles, and ospreys. Admission to the park is $1.00 per vehicle. The visitor center at the dam is open every day from 8:00 A.M. to 4:00 P.M., year-round. The park's visitor center is open Monday through Friday 8:00 A.M. to 4:00 P.M. For information call (800) CALL–WVA or (304) 269–0523.

About 15 miles east of Stonewall Jackson Lake is the community of ***Buckhannon,*** nestled in the foothills of the Alleghenies. It's a small town with a surprising number of unusual attractions. One of the first is ***West Virginia Wesleyan College,*** the largest private institution of higher learning in the state. Take a stroll around the beautiful, century-old, Georgian-style campus near the Buckhannon River and recall your school days. Be sure to duck into the gorgeous *Wesley Chapel,* a classic Greek Revival structure that seats 1,600 worshippers, making it the largest church in the state. The chapel, with its signature white steeple and Casavant organ with 1,500 pipes, holds regular religious services as well as special performing arts events, lectures, and community activities. The adjacent rhododendron garden blooms spectacularly in the late spring and early summer. During the tour you may also notice the modern Rockefeller Athletic Center, named for WVWC's former president Jay Rockefeller, also once the governor of West Virginia and now a U.S. senator. Campus tours are available, and reservations are requested. To make arrangements call (304) 473–8510.

Nearby you'll find another college, but this one is for our four-legged friends. *West Virginia Canine College,* on Evunbreath Road, is where some of the nation's best-trained dogs learned how to search for drugs and detect bombs. Graduates go on to such prestigious institutions as the Bureau of Alcohol, Tobacco and Firearms; the FBI; and the U.S. Customs Department. Humans also attend classes here to learn about training and breeding their furry friends. Call ahead, preferably a day in advance, for tour information at (304) 472–6691.

If you're in Buckhannon in May, you're in luck—the city's most anticipated event is forthcoming. *The Strawberry Festival* promotes the harvesting of the local crop of strawberries. This week-long event includes a parade with bands from all over the United States, dozens of floats, and even a Strawberry Queen and her court that float down Strawberry Lane. Tons of strawberries are served every imaginable way—and then some. You'll also find the usual festival food fare along with music and scores of craft exhibits, antique cars, and sports competitions. For more information on the citywide festival, call the West Virginia Strawberry Festival at (304) 472–9036.

Two miles north of town is another unusual attraction—a tree with a great story. At the spot where Turkey Run Creek enters the Buckhannon River (just off Route 119), look for *The Pringle Tree.* This large, hollow, sycamore tree is the third generation of one that provided shelter for two brothers, John and Samuel Pringle, who had deserted from the British army. The brothers ran from Fort Pitt (now Pittsburgh) in 1761 and on finding the tree in 1764, lived in its cavernous base for more than three years before venturing away from the area for ammunition. When they discovered the war was over, they returned to civilization but soon came back to the area to show others where they had lived in the wild. As legend goes, the party was so impressed by the bounty of the land, they decided to settle the area, making the spot the first permanent settlement west of the Alleghenies in Virginia. The tree is symbolic of the movement into the western frontier.

Pringle Tree Park is open from May 1 to November 1 during daylight hours. The park has picnic grounds, a playground, bathroom facilities, and a boat launch. Call the Upshur County Chamber of Commerce at (304) 472–1722 for more information.

The Pringle Tree

Just south of Buckhannon on Route 20 is the community of *French Creek* and the *West Virginia State Wildlife Center.* The history of the center is piecemeal, but it has roots in a game farm established on this 329-acre tract during the 1920s. The original facilities were beyond renovation, so an entirely new exhibit area was designed and built beginning in 1984.

Today visitors to the center can see elk, bison, mountain lions, timber wolves, white-tailed deer, black bears, coyotes, river otters, and many species of birds, all native to the state, in their natural habitat. A 1.25-mile loop walkway through the habitat is lined with interpretive signs to help you learn more about the animals and their impact on West Virginia history.

Enjoy the picnic area, then take a walk to the stocked pond to see trout, bass, catfish, and bluegill. The park is still growing, too. Already plans have been made for an educational and interpretive center, auditorium, nocturnal animal exhibit, reptile exhibit, and aquarium. The park is open April 1 through November 30. Hours are 9:00 A.M. to dusk, year-round. Admission is $2.00 for adults, $1.00 for children three to fifteen. Younger children are free. For information call (304) 924–6211.

Only 4 miles away is another not-to-be-missed brush with nature, especially if you're traveling with children. *Gate Farmpark,* in tiny Rock Cave, is a petting zoo with a twist—most of the animals are exotics. Children can get up close to the llamas, which they'll learn are gentle and clean animals. They might even hear a mother humming to her babies. Also popular are the adorable—and odorless—pot-bellied pigs from Southeast Asia, the pygmy goats, and the unusual horned Jacob sheep. The sheep, sporting as many as six horns, are as gentle as any breed of sheep. They're originally from Great Britain, where they've been bred as ornamental animals for estates for more than 350 years. Today, more than 100 breeders worldwide, including Jo-Ann and Frank Gate, continue the commitment to conserve this rare and distinctive animal. Gate Farmpark also has a country store, picnic area, and playground. It's open weekends only in May, September, and October. From Memorial Day weekend to Labor Day weekend, the park is open seven days a week, 10:00 A.M. to dusk. Call (304) 924–6176 for more information.

If you're fortunate enough to be in Central West Virginia in mid-March, then by all means head over to the aptly named Lewis County town of *Ireland,* about 10 miles west of Rock Cave. By the second week of March, most West Virginia fields are beginning to green—a rich, dark green, reminiscent of the rolling hills of the Emerald Isle itself. In the town of Ireland, the locals are celebrating their Celtic roots with one of the state's most festive Irish festivals. The week-long *Irish Spring Festival,* usually starting around the 15th of the month and always including St. Patrick's Day, is alive with so-called pot o'luck dinners, Irish gospel choirs, leprechaun contests, Irish jig contests, bike tours, parade, kite-flying contest, Mulligan stew cook-offs, and many more distinctively Irish pastimes.

Ireland, like most of West Virginia and the Southern Appalachians, was settled by Irish and Scottish pioneers, many of whom were ostracized by the British gentry who owned the sprawling plantations of the flatter and infinitely more fertile lowlands of Virginia, the Carolinas, and Georgia. Irelanders claim their community was first settled by an Irishman named Andrew Wilson, a gentleman who in his later years was known affectionately as "Old Ireland." According to local legend Wilson "lived to see 114 springtimes." When folks from around the countryside learned of this long life, many were convinced that there was something about the quality of life in Ireland—West Virginia—that was conducive to long life. Hence the town grew in numbers and prestige. Today it's home to 200 souls, but the population more than doubles during the festival. The town also receives a deluge of cards and letters from around the country to be postmarked "Ireland" for St. Patrick's Day. For more information on the festival, contact the Lewis County Convention and Visitors Bureau at (304) 269–7328.

Lodging is somewhat scarce along the backroads of Central West Virginia, so you might want to take a spin over to *Holly River State Park,* located just off Route 20 on the northern tip of Webster County. Nine fully equipped modern cabins are interspersed among the lushly forested hills and along the namesake river, which offers tremendous trout fishing in the spring and fall. The park also has a restaurant, visitor center, pool, and game courts. If you're looking for a more primitive experience, Holly River has eighty-eight campsites, all wooded and private with outdoor fireplaces and grills. Don't leave the park without hiking over to the scenic Upper Falls and Water Chute, part of Fall Run, which empties into Holly River. Call (304) 493–6353.

About 20 miles northwest of Buckhannon, and maybe a ten-minute drive north of Weston, is another charmingly named community in Lewis County, *Jane Lew.* The town is named after Jane Lewis, mother of Lewis Maxwell, one of the founders of Weston and a man who bought most of the land where this present-day burgh sits. In town, on Route 19 and Depot Street, you'll come across **The Glass Swan,** a shop offering hand-blown glassware as beautiful and delicate as its name. In the studio you can watch glassware being blown and decorated by meticulous artisans. Exhibitions are given daily Monday through Saturday. Times may vary so call ahead at (304) 884–8014. The studio is open May through August, 9:00 A.M. to 2:00 P.M., and September through April, 9:00 A.M. to 3:00 P.M. The retail store is open 9:00 A.M. to 5:00 P.M., Monday through Saturday.

Also in Jane Lew, on Route 19 North, is **Astolat Garden Perennials,** the place to go for local ornamental grasses, ferns, and flowers. You can browse the half-acre display gardens and cut your own bouquet. The staff here is happy to provide visitors with advice on plant selection and culture, garden design, and maintenance. The gardens are open May through October, Tuesday through Sunday, noon to sundown. Call (304) 884–8163 for more information.

Three miles west of Jane Lew is **Jackson's Mill Historic Area,** the boyhood home of Confederate legend General Thomas "Stonewall" Jackson.

Few foods are more regional in style, presentation, and taste than barbecue. South of the Mason-Dixon Line, the word barbecue is used only as a noun. In West Virginia and throughout most of the Mid-Atlantic region, barbecue is defined as chopped smoked pork served on a bun, with coleslaw and a vinegar-based sauce. In West Virginia, the coleslaw isn't a side item as it would be at a Texas barbecue restaurant. Rather, it's served right on top of the pork, inside the sandwich. Strange but tasty. Equally strange and tasty is a West Virginia hot dog with the works, which I first sampled in a hole-in-the-wall barbecue drive-through in Sutton, a place whose name long ago escaped me. I figured a hot dog with "the works" meant mustard, onions and relish. In Central West Virginia, "the works" means all that plus coleslaw. If that sounds less than appealing, suspend your doubts long enough to try one. Like the barbecue, you'll be surprised. You might even want seconds.

His grandparents settled the land and built the area's first gristmill along the banks of the West Fork River. Their son Cummins, Thomas's uncle, took possession of the property at the death of his father and ran the lucrative business, which included two mills, carpenter and blacksmiths shops, and a store. Thomas came to live with Cummins and his family in 1830 after the death of his parents, Jonathan and Julia. He left in 1842 for West Point and a brilliant military career.

The Jackson compound was also an important part of life for the entire surrounding area. Because of the Jackson family's interest in politics and the importance of their mill to the area economy, the homestead became a gathering place for area settlers.

Today the 523-acre park is open for tours and features *Jackson's Mill Museum,* a gristmill dating from 1841. The structure itself is amazing: The 2½-story wooden building, sitting on a stone foundation, is made out of lumber produced from the original foundation.

Don't miss the half-hour film on the life of Stonewall Jackson; then feel free to wander amid the artifacts, tools, and other items remaining from another era. See the apple butter kettle, the chicken watering jug, the varmint trap, and cheese press, among other authentic curios.

Also of interest on the property is *Blaker Mill* and the *McWhorter Cabin.* The mill, disassembled stone by stone from another part of the county and moved to its new location at Jackson's Mill, will eventually be a fully operating gristmill. Today you can see nineteenth-century technology at work as locally grown grains, actually used in the conference center's (see later) kitchen, are ground and even sold to the public.

The 200-year-old, hand-hewn, log McWhorter cabin, also relocated here, was the handiwork of Henry McWhorter, a New Yorker who had served in the Revolutionary War before moving south. He and his family lived in the one-room cabin for thirty-seven years. It is located on the original site where the Jackson home once stood. Admission is $2.00 for adults, $1.00 for children under twelve. Jackson's Mill is open Memorial Day through Labor Day, noon to 5:00 P.M. Closed Mondays. For information call (304) 269–5100.

If you're near Jackson's Mill in the summer, stay around for one of the best festivals anywhere in the United States. Usually around Labor Day weekend, hundreds of artisans gather here for the *Stonewall Jackson Heritage Arts and Crafts Jubilee* to exhibit traditional Appalachian handcrafts. Blown and stained glass, pottery, quilts and dolls, handmade lace, and dozens of other items are displayed here.

Crafters aren't the only ones who show up. This is one of the state's premier mountain music show-cases. Singers and musicians from around the region put on quite a show with mountain dulcimers, guitars, banjos, and fiddles echoing through the hills deep into the night, along with the stomping of square dancers. History buffs, meanwhile, will enjoy the eerily realistic battle reenactments, while rugged outdoorsmen will be in awe of the wood-

Jackson's Mill

chopping demonstration, in which hearty men and women slice through native hardwoods as if they were butter. With all that gawking you'll be doing, you'll need sustenance. Mouthwatering vittles are every-where, including pork barbecue sandwiches, catfish platters, cobblers, cornbread and beans, pancakes, barbecued chicken, and ice cream made on the spot. A four-day pass is $8.00 for adults, or $4.00 per day. Children's passes are $1.00 and those under twelve are free. Call (800) 296–1863 or (304) 269–1863 Monday through Friday, 9:00 A.M. to 4:00 P.M., for information.

When you're through enjoying the historic area at Jackson's Mill, it's time to take in the park's more modern amenities. Today it has a beau-tiful stone *Conference Center* providing year-round activities for those seeking to get away from the office or simply to take a vacation. Origi-nally a youth camp (this was the site of the nation's first state 4-H camp, established in 1921), it now has a contemporary twenty-three-room stone lodge and fourteen cottages to house guests. Various private rooms also are scattered around the campus. More than twenty-five meeting facilities are available for groups as large as 500 or as few as 10. Accessibility isn't a problem, either; the center has an airstrip, built in 1935 and improved later when the Navy trained pilots here.

The food at the conference center is enough to entice you to stay. *Jack-son's Mill Restaurant* offers hearty home-cooked meals, served family style, three times a day. Bakers offer hot, fresh biscuits, coffee cake, and succulent cream puffs. Entrées include pasta, fresh green salads with homemade dressing, New York strip steaks, deep-fried chicken, and Virginia ham. You can work dinner off by visiting the camp's *gift shop*; playing basketball, volleyball, tennis, or horseshoes; or going for a swim. The historic area is just a short walk away.

Rates are very reasonable, and in the off season are offered at 70 percent off for Sunday through Friday morning stays. For information call (304) 269–5100.

When you're ready to leave, get back on I–79 and go north into Harrison County for a look at what early American farm life was like. Between Lost Creek and West Milford lies *Watters Smith Homestead,* a 523-acre farm established in 1796 on land originally patented by Patrick Henry and owned by four generations of the Watters Smith family, early pioneers in this region. It still contains a hand-hewn eighteenth-century livestock barn, carpenter and blacksmith shops, a modest 120-year-old home built by a Smith family descendant, and a small museum with frontier farm equipment. Start at the visitors center, then take the self-guided tour. After you've learned a bit of history, cool off in the swimming pool located in the park's recreation area. Docent tours are conducted from 11:00 A.M. to 7:00 P.M. every day of the week from Memorial Day through Labor Day. Tours at other times of the year are available by reservation only. Small donations are accepted. Call (304) 842–7272 or (800) 368–4324.

From here, you're only about 10 miles south of Clarksburg, one of the prettiest and most historic cities in the state. Just off the interstate, it's at the intersection of Routes 19 and 50. Clarksburg was established in 1785 and is, among other things, the birthplace of native son Stonewall Jackson. One of the best places to get started on your tour of the city is downtown at *Waldomore,* a Greek Revival nineteenth-century mansion that houses historical information on West Virginia history and culture. It's chock-full of museum-quality pieces from the mid-1800s and holds works by local authors and historical documents from the life and times of Stonewall Jackson.

Also of note at Waldomore is the *Gray Barker UFO Collection,* one of the nation's largest UFO exhibits, featuring documents from investigations and sightings as well as a slew of provocative photographs, official records, and correspondence among various international UFO societies. As you might imagine, West Virginia's rural nature—and amazingly dark nighttime skies—make it a rich fodder ground for all things UFO. Buckhannon native Gray Barker amassed this large personal collection, and after his death Waldomore assembled it into a museum-quality collection, one that attracts folks from around the world. Waldomore and the Gray Barker UFO Collection are open Tuesday, Wednesday, and Friday, 9:00 A.M. to 5:00 P.M.; Thursday, 1:00 P.M. to 8:00 P.M.; and Saturday, 9:00 A.M. to noon. Call (304) 624–6512.

Also in the 16-block downtown historic district is the *Stealey-Goff-Vance House,* 123 West Main Street, with its large collection of Indian artifacts and the impressive bronze sculpture, *The Immigrants,* a tribute to the Belgian, Czech, Greek, Hungarian, Irish, Italian, Romanian, and Spanish immigrants who came to the Clarksburg area during the 1880s to work in the glass factories and coalfields. The monument, on Main Street on the courthouse grounds, conveys the spirit in which these diverse immigrants pulled together to form a harmonious community that still exists today.

West of Clarksburg on Route 50 is the town of *Salem,* settled in 1792. This is a little city with an unusual history. It was settled by Seventh-Day Baptist families from New Jersey after a two-and-a-half-year journey westward in search of religious freedom. Their legacy lives on at *Fort New Salem,* a reconstructed Appalachian pioneer settlement now under

Twinkle, Twinkle . . .

*A*s inspiring as the scenery is in West Virginia during the day, it can be even more awesome after the sun sets.

After the canoes are pulled ashore, dinner is over, and the fire has died down, it's time to kick back and watch the stars. The first thing you notice, aside from the incredible display of constellations, is the absolute quiet of the evening countryside. For the unaccustomed urban dweller, it can even be borderline eerie, or so I'm told.

Looking up at the heavens, the thought inevitably runs through your head . . . "if there's anything to that UFO business, this is the kind of place where

you're bound to see one." And, if you just so happen to spot anything unusual in the West Virginia skies, you wouldn't be the first to do so. Quite a few West Virginians and other travelers through the state have claimed to have had close encounters—hence the Gray Barker UFO Collection in Clarksburg (see page 120).

Whether you see anything suspicious or not, a few minutes of restful, meditative stargazing in West Virginia won't leave you disappointed. It's a pretty magnificent place to take in the grandeur of the universe, one twinkle at a time.

the patronage of nearby Salem-Teikyo University, just a mile away. Each year thousands of visitors come to enjoy this living-history museum, and some even stay to get college degrees. The university, which is aligned with Japan's Teikyo University, offers a master of arts degree in education, with an emphasis in Appalachian folk life. Public workshops are offered by the university at the settlement, and some of the fort buildings double as classroooms for Appalachian studies students.

Printing, weaving, blacksmithing, quilting, cooking, and other tasks are demonstrated at the fort regularly. Start your meandering at *The Sign of the 3 Barrels,* a visitors center and store. Then see the *Blockhouse* and the *Meeting House,* used for church services, trails, and school. Then head over to *Delila's House,* a good example of what slave quarters were like in 1815. And don't miss the *Apothecary,* which offers a fine demonstration of how early settlers cured themselves when there weren't any doctors around. For example: aloe vera for burns, lavender to cure colds. Also on the tour are a print shop, the farmhouse, and the *Green Tree Tavern,* where the locals come to gossip.

Depending on the time of the year, the fort, which is actually West Virginia's answer to Jamestown, is alive with celebrations and demonstrations. Festivals honor Appalachian traditions year-round, including an old-fashioned Christmas celebration each December.

Admission is $3.50 for adults, $2.00 for children ages six to twelve, and children under six get in free. It's open on April 24 (for Folk Fair), then April 26 through May 21, Monday through Friday, 10:00 A.M. to 5:00 P.M. Memorial Day through October 31, Wednesday through Friday, hours are 10:00 A.M. to 5:00 P.M., and Saturday and Sunday 1:00 to 5:00 P.M. For further information call (304) 782–5245.

After a full day at New Salem, jump back on Route 50 and head east past Clarksburg to the little town of *Bridgeport.* Founded as a trading post in 1764, it still serves as a good spot to stop for a rest and bite to eat. There are a number of national chain hotels/motels and restaurants along the highway, but for a real taste of local flavor, go shopping!

Sample the local retail scene by stopping at *Shalady's,* a three-story antiques store filled to the rafters with quality glassware, art, housewares, and collectibles. It's downtown, where there is quite a jumble of intriguing shops. Call (304) 842–6691. Also nearby is the *Hospitality Shop,* 910 West Main Street. Candles, brass, pewter, baskets, country furniture, and other home furnishings line the shelves here. Call (304) 842–4215.

Don't spend all your money at Shalady's, however. You'll want to save a few coins to give to the folks at *Heritage Arts & Crafts Village,* at I–79, Stonewood exit. Housed in the old Quiet Dell School, this is the state's largest artisan's cooperative, rich with handmade quilts, stained glass, baskets, pottery, and dolls made by local artists. If your interests go beyond just admiring and purchasing the handiworks, you might want to look into taking one of several arts classes held throughout the year at Heritage. Course include basketweaving, ceramics, and stained-glass making. Call (800) 524–4043 or 622–3304 for information.

Now put away those shopping bags and head south on Route 76 into beautiful Barbour County. There's lots of water here, notably from the lower half of gigantic Tygart Lake. *Audra State Park,* south of the lake off of U.S. 119, contains the beautiful Middle Fork River, with its gigantic rocks for sunbathing and its clear, cool water for diving. Meandering back to the north on U.S. 250 places you in Philippi, the Barbour County seat. This is where you'll find a treasure of another kind—*Philippi Bridge,* one of the prettiest covered bridges in the country and certainly the most scenic south of New England. The bridge is located just west of town on U.S. 119/250 and spans the width of the Tygart River. It's the only structure of its kind that is still a part of a federal highway, and is also the state's oldest covered bridge, built in 1852. North and South fought the first land battle of the Civil War on June 3, 1861, over this bridge. The battle, known in these parts as the Philippi Races, was an easy victory for the Union forces. For more information call (304) 457–1225.

PLACES TO STAY IN CENTRAL WEST VIRGINIA

SUMMERSVILLE
Sleep Inn,
U.S. 19 North;
(304) 872–4500

Comfort Inn,
U.S. 19 North;
(304) 872–6500

BUCKHANNON
Post Mansion Inn,
8 Island Avenue;
(304) 472–8959

Colonial Hotel,
North Kanawha Street;
(304) 472–3000

Bicentennial Motel,
90 East Main Street;
(304) 472–5000

Deer Park inn and Lodge,
Heavener Grove Road;
(800) 296–8430

WESTON
Jackson's Mill State 4-H
Conference Center,
U.S. 19 North;
(304) 269–5100

CLARKSBURG
Holiday Inn,
100 Lodgeville Road;
(304) 842–5411

PLACES TO EAST IN CENTRAL WEST VIRGINIA

SUMMERSVILLE
Shoney's,
U.S. 19 North;
(304) 872–6785

Western Steer,
U.S. 19 North;
(304) 872–5638

BUCKHANNON
Deer Park inn and Lodge,
Heavener Grove Road;
(800) 296–8430

Main Street Cafe
and Tavern,
90 East Main Street;
(304) 472–5000

WESTON
Jackson's Mill Restaurant,
U.S. 19 North;
(304) 269–5100

CLARKSBURG
Churchill's Grille
(Holiday Inn),
100 Lodgeville Road;
(304) 842–5411

FOR MORE INFORMATION

Clarksburg Convention and
Visitors Bureau;
(304) 842–7272

Buckhannon/Upshur
County Convention and
Visitors Bureau; (304)
472–1722

Lewis County Convention
and Visitors Bureau;
(304) 269–7328

Northern West Virginia

Like neighboring Pennsylvania, Northern West Virginia is a region of intensive mining, industry, and agriculture. It's an oddly shaped region that includes the Northern Panhandle (whose northernmost point is actually closer to Canada than it is to the southern border of West Virginia), the greater Morgantown area, and the bucolic countryside of Preston, Taylor, and Marion counties.

Northern West Virginia, probably because of its industrial and coal-mining heritage, is also the most ethnically diverse part of the state, with particularly large Italian and Polish populations. Of course, ethnic festivals and eateries are popular here, and the astute traveler won't ever leave hungry.

With industrial Wheeling as its northern hub and collegiate, pastoral Morgantown as its southern gateway, Northern West Virginia represents a pretty good microcosm of all of West Virginia. And perhaps for that reason alone, this makes for a good place to cap off a statewide tour.

The Northern Heartland

Rich soil and scenery define this quiet corner of Northern West Virginia, which covers all of Preston, Taylor, and Marion Counties. From the south, the gateway to the region is **Grafton,** a tranquil tree-lined community perched on the upper shores of Tygart Lake. Like most of the towns in the area, Grafton emerged along a wilderness road that opened this part of the Mountain State to civilization in the East. What is now U.S. Route 50—the brainchild of French engineering genius Claude Crozet—runs through the middle of town. Crozet surveyed and blazed much of the wilderness road (which now extends from Maryland to California) and is credited with being one of the founders of Grafton.

Perhaps the most interesting sidelight here is a shrine that will go straight to the heart of any good mother and child. It's the **International Mother's Day Shrine,** located at Andrews Methodist Church on Main Street, about a mile south of the Route 50/U.S. 119 intersection.

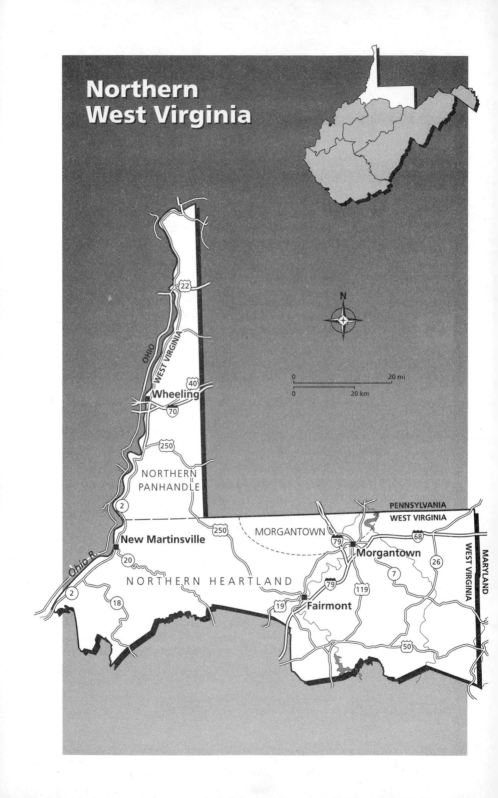

NORTHERN WEST VIRGINIA

BEST ANNUAL EVENTS IN
NORTHERN WEST VIRGINIA

Grafton native Anna Jarvis is credited with organizing the first celebration of Mother's Day at the pretty redbrick church in 1908. Miss Jarvis, who was living in Philadelphia at the time, thought it would be a nice gesture to have the church where her mother taught Sunday school for more than twenty years recognize the first "Mother's Day" on the third anniversary of her mom's death, which happened to fall on the second Sunday in May. The first local observance was held at Grafton church that year. Six years later, in 1914, at the request of Miss Jarvis, a resolution calling for a national observance of Mother's Day was passed by both houses of Congress and approved by President Woodrow Wilson.

The International Mother Day's Shrine, depicting a mother, infant, and small child, was erected adjacent to the 122-year-old church in 1962. A special Mother's Day service is held at the church on that day each year at 2:30 P.M. Guided tours of the historic church and grounds are available year-round by special appointment. The church is also open to the public from April 15 through October every Monday through Friday, 9:30 A.M. to 3:30 P.M. Call (304) 265–1589.

West Virginia University Mountaineer Football, Morgantown; September through December; (800) CALL–WVA

Mountaineer Country Glass Festival, Morgantown; mid-June; (304) 599–3550

Jamboree in the Hills, Wheeling; late July; (304) 234–0050

Mason-Dixon Festival, Morgantown; late September; (304) 599–1104

Mountaineer Balloon Festival, Morgantown; early October; (304) 296–8356

Oglebayfest, Wheeling; early October; (304) 243–4010

Winter Festival of Lights, Wheeling, November through early January; (304) 243–4010.

There's another important shrine in Grafton, albeit of a different sort. The ***Grafton National Cemetery*** is the final resting place for 1,251 Union and Confederate soldiers who fell victim to the violent clashes that broke out near Grafton, which was a strategic railroad center connecting the interior of West Virginia with Union supply and industrial plants in Parkersburg and Wheeling. Among those buried here was Private Bailey Brown, the first Union soldier killed in the Civil War. The beautiful, maple-draped cemetery, dedicated in 1867, is open to the public year-round from dawn to dusk.

From Grafton, head east a few miles on Route 50 into scenic Preston County, which sits high on the Alleghany Plateau, a region of rich farmland and tiny tucked-away villages. One of the first such hamlets you'll come upon is Evansville, home of the ***Maurice Jennings Museum,*** a small but eclectic collection of vintage antiques and cars. In the same building, located on Route 50, is the Sycamore Kitchen Restaurant, a very nice spot to grab a Sunday afternoon lunch of traditional, hearty country fare. In fact, Sunday is the only time to grab lunch here; both the museum and the restaurant are open only on Sundays. Call (304) 892–3225.

Just a mile farther down the road, in Fellowsville, sits **Conn's Grocery,** a quintessential West Virginia country store and a great place to pick up some picnic supplies, fishing bait, and a whole lot of country gossip. Conn's has been around since 1940, and it shows no signs of surrendering to the Wal-Marts and Safeways. Call (304) 892–3917.

After you've grabbed some fishing line, a bobber, and some fresh nightcrawlers, it's time to head over to the trout pond at Fellowsville's **Cool Springs Park,** also located on Route 50 just at the base of rugged Laurel Mountain. At the park you'll find a display of antique farm implements, including fascinating old tractors and threshing machines, reminders of the county's agricultural roots. The park's Old Water Wheel Restaurant serves up a tasty hamburger, and after your meal you can browse through the adjoining gift shop, which is full of local arts and crafts.

From the park, continue east on Route 50 for about another 20 miles to majestic **Cathedral State Park,** certainly one of West Virginia's most unusual natural attractions. Before the timber barons of the early twentieth century began exploiting the state's vast forests of pine and hardwoods, much of the West Virginia wilderness once looked like Cathedral State Park, a dense canopy of towering, awesome trees. This 132-acre reserve, open for day-use only, contains virgin hemlocks and hardwoods, some measuring more than 10 feet in diameter and over 100-feet tall. It's West Virginia's finest primeval forest, and because of its location right off of Route 50, it's also one of the nation's most accessible old-growth forests.

The trees, incidentally, were spared during the timber boom because they were on private property, a mountain resort. Later the land was donated to the state. Among the park's many ancient trees is a centennial hemlock, a 500-year-old beauty with a circumference of 21 feet and measuring 121 feet tall. Among the park's maze of well-manicured trails, you'll come across imposing stands of yellow birch, red oak, black cherry, maple, chestnut, and beech. As you might imagine, the scene here during the mid-October foliage season is unforgettable.

Cathedral State Park is about a mile east of the town of Aurora. It's open year-round from 6:00 A.M. to 10:00 P.M. Guided park ranger tours are given once a week, typically Wednesday, from spring through fall, but call ahead for hours and special programs (304–735–3771).

NORTHERN WEST VIRGINIA

BEST ATTRACTIONS IN NORTHERN WEST VIRGINIA

Jamboree U.S.A.,
Wheeling; (304) 234–0050

Independence Hall,
Wheeling; (304) 238–1300

Wheeling Artisan Center,
Wheeling; (304) 233–5330

Valley Falls State Park,
Fairmont; (304) 367–2719

*Cheat River Whitewater
Rafting,* throughout the
region; (800) CALL–WVA

*West Virginia Public
Theatre,* Morgantown;
(304) 598–0144

Sagebrush Round-Up,
Fairmont; (304) 366–4864

After a hike through Cathedral, you might come away feeling a bit spiritual. Hold on to that sensation because just down the road in Horse Shoe Run is *Our Lady of the Pines,* supposedly the smallest church in forty-eight states and one of the smallest Roman Catholic churches in the world. The 16-foot-by-11-foot stone structure, with six West Virginia–made stained-glass windows, a tiny altar, and six pews, can seat at best a dozen worshippers. It was built in the late 1950s by a local family and today is visited by thousands each year who come to pray, walk the beautiful grounds, and send postcards from the adjacent post office, also one of the smallest anywhere.

Our Lady of the Pines is open daily during daylight hours from spring through fall. The church is tucked away on a small knoll within earshot of State Route 24, about 6 miles south of Route 50. There is no admission charge—though donations are welcome—and there is no phone.

Every great river starts with a trickle from a spring. The Potomac River is no exception. About 6 miles south of Horse Shoe Run is the source spring of the mighty Potomac, a river that serves as a border between West Virginia and Maryland for more than 100 miles. Marking the spot of the spring is *Fairfax Stone,* a boundary point established by the wealthy British colonist Thomas Lord Fairfax. The spring marked the northwestern border of Fairfax's land holdings, a vast real estate empire that included what is now almost half of Virginia and most of the West Virginia Eastern Panhandle. You can visit this spot and pay homage to Fairfax and the river that would go on to define so much of these states. It's located 6 miles south of Silver Lake off a gravel road off of U.S. 219 (look for the sign on 219) in a remote stretch of country that must have looked much the same when Fairfax himself was surveying the area. The Fairfax Stone State Monument is open year-round dawn to dusk. However, do not try to negotiate this road in heavy snowfall. The marker is actually a couple of miles down the gravel road, and if you get stuck there's not a whole lot of traffic coming in or out of this way-off-the-beaten-path site.

Isolation and poverty have long been associated with the largely impenetrable hills and hollows of West Virginia. As such, the state has seen its share of social engineering experiments, including the nation's first federal New Deal homestead, **Arthurdale.** This western Preston County community, about 35 miles northwest of Fairfax Stone, was the pet project of then first lady Eleanor Roosevelt. The federal home-steading plan she help craft served two purposes: to provide affordable, quality housing and to help boost the Depression era economy of America's rural areas. Arthurdale became the prototype community, with more than 165 houses built here during 1933. All of the original homes are still intact in this proud and tidy community. In addition a few of the original homesteading families, many of whom came from urban areas of the Northeast, remain.

Now part of the National Register of Historic Places, Arthurdale makes for an interesting driving tour. You can get maps and other materials at the town's administration building/visitor center, which is open in the summer months from noon to 5:00 P.M. on Saturday and 2:00 P.M. to 5:00 P.M. on Sunday. Arthurdale is located on State Route 92, 3 miles south of the State Route 7 junction. Special tours are available year-round by appointment. Call Arthurdale Heritage, Inc., at (304) 864–3959 for more information.

Virtually splitting Preston County into two equal halves is the **Cheat River,** which comes out of the mountains of the Potomac Highlands and flows north through the state before emptying into Cheat Lake and ultimately the Monongahela River north of Morgantown.

The Cheat, with its boulder-strewn shoreline and glaciated gorges, is easily the premier white-water river in Northern West Virginia and per-haps third in the state, behind only the Gauley and New Rivers. Conse-quently the area has attracted several professional river outfitters. For rafting trips on the Cheat, as well as the Potomac, Shenandoah, and other fabled rivers of this region, hook up with either **Appalachian Wildwaters/USA Raft** (304–454–2475) in nearby Rowlesburg or **Cheat River Outfitters** (304–329–2024) in Albright. Both outfitters offer a range of trips, including overnight, weekend, and extended camping trips. Late spring trips tend to be the most exciting (because of the high water levels) and are often the most crowded.

When the hunger pangs hit, head west to Fairmont, the seat of Marion County, and get ready for an epicurean masterpiece. **Muriale's,** 1742 Fairmont Avenue, on the south side of town, is probably the best Italian restaurant in the state. The local landmark is famous for its huge portions of wonderful lasagna, ravioli, rigatoni, spaghetti, and cavatelli. Included in the *Who's Who in America's Restaurants,* Muriale's is testament to North-ern West Virginia's rich Italian heritage. With six separate dining rooms, it's a family-friendly kind of place that attracts regular diners from as far away as Pennsylvania and Maryland. Although the star attraction is the pasta, made fresh on the premises, Muriale's also serves hearty steaks, hoagies, pizza, and a wide variety of seafood. It's open daily year-round (except Christmas) from 11:00 A.M. to 9:00 P.M. A massive Sunday buffet, an attraction in itself, is served starting at 9:00 A.M. Call (304) 363–3190.

West Augusta Historical Society Round Barn

If you've already paid homage to mothers by visiting the International Mother's Day Shrine in Grafton, now you've got your chance to salute fathers. Following Grafton's lead, Fairmont's Central United Methodist Church, 301 Fairmont Avenue, was the site of the first observance of Father's Day on July 5, 1908. You can even have your Father's Day cards imprinted here with a special stamp. The so-called *Father's Day Church* is available for tours by calling (304) 366–3351.

Immediately west of Fairmont is the small community of Monongah, a coal mining town that was the scene of a devastating mine explosion that killed 361 men in 1907. The victims of this tragedy—and others like it that too often plagued the Mountain State—are remembered at the West Virginia *Miner's Memorial,* a moving bronze sculpture located in Mary Lou Retton Park, named in honor of the famous Olympic Gold Medal winner and Marion County native. The park, located just off of U.S. 19, is open daily from dawn to dusk.

The gently rolling countryside around Fairmont is dotted with beautiful dairy farms and pastureland. Agriculture is still an important part of the economy, and here you can trace its colorful roots by visiting the *West Augusta Historical Society Round Barn* in Mannington, 10 miles west of Fairmont on U.S. 250. The striking round, wooden barn, commonly known as the Mannington Round Barn, was built as a dairy barn in 1912 by Amos Hamilton. Its unique architecture was commonplace on dairy farms in Pennsylvania, West Virginia, and Virginia during the late 1800s and early 1900s. This particular barn is the only such restored structure in the state and one of the few remaining south of the Mason-Dixon line.

OTHER ATTRACTIONS WORTH SEEING IN NORTHERN WEST VIRGINIA

Jamboree U. S. A.—
Wheeling

Brooke Glass Company—
Wellsburg

Wheeling Downs—
Wheeling

Valley Falls State Park—
Fairmont

Coopers Rock State Forest—
Bruceton Mills

Most round barns, including this one, were built into the side of a small hill, enabling the farmer to drive a hay wagon directly into the loft from the rear. Farmer Hamilton's round barn not only sheltered cows and feed but was also the main residence for the family. Your tour will undoubtedly start in the kitchen and wend around the three stories of living space, which is now full of family heirlooms and farm artifacts—milk coolers, lard presses, butter churns, a children's sleigh, carriage, and a horse-drawn potato picker. There are even some early West Virginia coal mining tools on display.

The round barn is open on Sundays, May through September, 1:30 P.M. to 4:00 P.M. Special tours also can be arranged any time of the year for small groups. In addition the barn hosts a ladies' quilting exhibition every Thursday from 9:00 A.M. to 2:00 P.M. A small donation is requested. For more information contact the historical society at (304) 986–2636 or 986–1089.

Morgantown

From Mannington, head east back into Fairmont and pick up U.S. 19 north to Morgantown. One of the most interesting communities in the Mountain State, Morgantown is a harmonic blend of blue bloods, blue collars, bohemians, and college students. It stands as its own subregion in this book because it's really unlike any other community in West Virginia. It is to the Mountain State what Austin is to Texas, Boulder is to Colorado, Madison is to Wisconsin. It's an industrial town with long ties to the nearby northern coalfields and famed glass factories, but it's also a high-tech town anchored by research laboratories maintained by the federal government. West Virginia University, with some 22,000 students spread across three separate campuses, keeps what would probably be a sleepy town lively year-round.

The university also provides a cultural backdrop that is probably unrivaled among West Virginia cities. The **WVU Creative Arts Center** schedules more than 300 music, theater, and performance art shows a year as well as a host of visual art exhibits. The centerpiece of the modern facility is the **Lakeview Theatre,** a large playhouse that stages both university shows and national touring productions. Tours and performance schedules can be had by calling (304) 293–4841. The center is located about a mile north of downtown off Beechurst Avenue on the Evansdale campus of the university.

Another interesting campus site is the *Core Arboretum,* run by the WVU biology department, featuring 3 miles of trails that wend through a forest of virtually every type of hardwood and pine tree native to West Virginia. Along the way you'll also see an amazing variety of wildflowers, shrubs, and decorative plants common to the state. It's located opposite the arts center on Beechurst. For special tours and bloom and foliage information, you can call the biology department at (304) 293–5201.

Probably the best way to get familiar with the campus, shy of going to school here or having a son or daughter attending, is by dropping in at the *WVU Visitors Center,* 120 Patterson Drive. The center offers a two-hour bus and walking tour of the three campuses, beginning with a short film. The student-led tour includes stops at all the major attractions, but along the way you'll also hear some good insider gossip and trivia about campus life and lore. For instance, on any given football Saturday afternoon, 70,000-seat Mountaineer Field becomes the single largest "city" in West Virginia.

If you happen to be in town during such an affair, by all means try to get tickets, but don't necessarily count on it. If you don't get them, take

Touchdown Mountaineers!

*I*n the Empire State, it's "The Big Apple." In California, it's "The City of Angels." Illinois boasts "The Windy City." Go down the list and you'll see that every state has its version of the "Big City." Yes, some West Virginians will even say they have one in Charleston, or perhaps Huntington. But in reality, the biggest city in West Virginia isn't a city at all. It's a football stadium filled to capacity on a gorgeous autumn afternoon. Of course, we're talking about the 70,000-seat Mountaineer Field on the campus of West Virginia University in Morgantown, a sporting shrine of sorts that holds at least 10,000 more people than the entire city of Charleston. While the Mountaineers may not win every time they take the field—although victories have been the norm in recent years—it's always a celebration in Morgantown on a football Saturday. If you plan to go, be wise and take a pair of earplugs . . . or two pairs. Decibel levels after a Mountaineer touchdown have been known to eclipse the noise level of a runway during a jet takeoff. We're not kidding.

After all, what big city isn't noisy?

advantage of the deserted downtown streets and hop into a local gallery, pub, or shop. *The Appalachian Gallery,* 160 Chancery Row, is known for its rotating exhibits of works by regional artists. Other great tucked-away spots include the **Art Attic,** 316 High Street, with its original fine-art prints, pottery, and hand-crafted jewelry and textiles, and *Garo,* 111 Walnut Street, a gallery with a surprisingly large selection of original graphic works, mostly from the late 1800s and early 1900s.

At the Old Post Office, 107 High Street, you can browse through the *Monongalia Arts Center.* Inside the neoclassical-style building, with its pronounced Doric engaged columns, is Benedum Gallery, housing touring exhibits from around the country. The adjoining Tanner Theater regularly stages plays and community events. The complex is open weekdays 9:00 A.M. to 4:00 P.M. and on weekends for special engagements. For more information call (304) 292–3325.

After some creative loafing, it might be time to refuel. If you've got a hankering for some sudsy sustenance, head over to *West Virginia Brewing Company,* 1291 University Avenue. It's billed as West Virginia's first and only brew pub (although we're not so sure about the latter claim anymore), but one fact that does hold up is that the handcrafted beers here are indeed outstanding. The collegiate types that pack the cozy bar are testament to that. Hours are 11:30 A.M. to 2:00 A.M. Monday through Saturday; closed Sunday. Call (304) 296–BREW.

Lightly populated West Virginia probably isn't the first place to come to mind when thinking of rapid-transit systems, but one of the best in the world can be found in *Morgantown.* It's the *Personal Rapid Transit,* or PRT, an electrically powered system that transports WVU students to classes across the three-campus university. (If you've ever ridden the People Mover at Disneyland, this is much the same concept.) The computer-automated cars, resembling small subway vehicles, whisk as many as twenty students per car at a time at a comfortable 30 miles per hour. Nearly 20,000 students ride the seventy-plus cars every day; the longest trips lasts just over ten minutes. The PRT stops on Walnut Street, Beechurst Avenue, and near the university's student housing complex, engineering department, and medical center. Studied by city planners, environmentalists, and transit officials worldwide, the twenty-year-old WVU system has transported more than forty-five million passengers without a single injury or a single carbohydron released into the air. Students ride the system for free, but visitors are also encouraged to hop aboard. Adults pay a $1.00 round-trip fee, a minimal fee considering this is one of the most interesting and relaxing ways to tour Morgantown and the university. The PRT is open Monday through Friday, 6:30 A.M. to 10:30 P.M., and Saturday, 9:30 A.M. to 5:00 P.M. It's closed Sundays and during university holidays. For more information call (304) 293–5011.

October, as mentioned throughout this book, is a wonderful time to tour West Virginia. In Morgantown it's especially enticing given that this is when the annual *Mountaineer Balloon Festival* lifts off. The color in the sky nearly matches the blazing foliage as dozens of hot-air balloons ascend and exceed the height of the surrounding mountains. Hart Field, a.k.a. Morgantown Municipal Airport, is the site of this festival, which also features an array of balloon races, carnival rides, music attractions,

A True West Virginian

*W*est Virginia's current governor, Cecil Underwood, is not your typical politician. Most West Virginians will tell you he's enjoyed a fairy-tale political life even before assuming office two years ago. This wasn't even his first stay in the Governor's Mansion, but it was a long time between visits. The seventy-five-year-old Republican was actually first elected back in 1956 at the ripe age of thirrty-four. At the time, he was the youngest elected governor not only in West Virginia history, but in American history as well. Underwood's political journey actually began, however, at the age of twenty-two when he was elected to the West Virginia House of Delegates. This precocious achievement even landed him on a popular 1950s television show, What's My Line.

I was privileged to interview Underwood back in the early 1990s, when he was a private citizen directing an initiative to attract high-tech industry to the Morgantown area. If I remember

right, the project was named "Software Valley," and it proved to be a somewhat fruitful effort.

What I do remember most from that interview in Underwood's unassuming Morgantown office was the governor's unbridled boosterism of the Mountain State. I asked him point blank if he still pined for higher political office, perhaps another shot at a Senate seat in Washington. (He was defeated in an earlier attempt in 1960.) "No, not really," he said. "There's so much more I can do right here in West Virginia. Besides, I'm not sure I could live in Washington, D.C. It's a beautiful city to visit, though," he said with a slight Southern drawl. I immediately tried a different tack and asked if he were ever to serve in Washington, what neighborhood in that city would he want to reside in. "Oh, that's easy. I'd live over in the Eastern Panhandle."

Spoken like a true West Virginian.

food booths, crafts, and games for the kids. The
fete is usually held in the middle of the month, a
time when the leaves in the surrounding countryside have reached their peak. In a state that's
brimming with festivals, this may be one of the
best. For exact dates call (304) 296–8356.

Spectacular as it is, you don't have to settle on
just watching the hot-air balloons from the
ground. Try flying in one! It's possible through
Fun Aviation, Inc., a balloon-flying service that'll take you up for an
hour-long champagne flight. (Don't worry, the passengers are the only
ones doing the drinking.) If you get really hooked, the Morgantown
company will also offer flight instruction classes. Fun Aviation is
located at 1105 Charles Avenue. Call (304) 291–2FLY.

After a busy day in Morgantown, you're going to need a place to rest
those tired bones. The charming **Hotel Morgan** is located in an old
brick building (circa 1925) at 127 High Street in the heart of downtown.
Nothing particularly fancy, the seven-story hotel nevertheless exudes a
sense of yesteryear with its creaky floors and old windows overlooking
the central business district. It's a somewhat intimate affair with only
forty rooms and a few suites. On football weekends, however, the place
can get a bit rowdy. Many of the rooms have kitchen suites and all have
cable TV and air-conditioning. In the morning grab a fresh pastry at
the hotel's Aunt Patty's Cafe. For reservations call (304) 292–8401.

For many West Virginia artisans, works that are not sold at craft shows
or other irregularly scheduled events too often gather dust in the back-
rooms of studios and houses. Tom Tanner, owner of **Crafter's Corner**
in the town of Hundred, about a half-hour drive west of Morgantown,
decided a couple of years ago to create a market for some local artisans
whom he thought had significant but underexposed talents. Today
Tanner's shop exhibits works from about two dozen craftspeople,
including folk toys, quilts, paintings, jewelry, stuffed animals, and floral arrangements. It's quite interesting "stuff," as Tanner likes to say,
and it's bolstered by the proprietor's own handmade wooden trains
and cradles. Tanner's operation is also a selfless endeavor. The store
takes only a 10 percent commission on works that it sells, and exhibits
are rotated once a week so that everyone gets equal representation.
Displays often feature different crafters' works mixed together,
because, according to Tanner, it is often the case that one person's work
helps sell another's. Crafters Corner is typically open Thursday

through Saturday from 9:00 A.M. to 5:00 P.M. and just about anytime by appointment. It's located at the intersection of U.S. 250 and State Route 69 in "downtown" Hundred.

While in Hundred, be sure to detour off U.S. 250 at County Road 13 and drive over the **Fish Creek Covered Bridge,** a 36-foot-long structure built in 1881 and spanning the namesake creek.

The Northern Panhandle

The four "Yankee" counties of West Virginia—Marshall, Ohio, Brooke, and Hancock—collectively make up the Northern Panhandle, a region whose northernmost point is closer to Canada than to the southern border of West Virginia. All of the Northern Panhandle lies north of the Mason-Dixon line, and the residents here tend to have strong affiliations with such nearby northeastern industrial cities as Pittsburgh and Cleveland. Although industrial, the Northern Panhandle is also surprisingly green with heavy forests, gentle hills, and fertile pastureland found along the Ohio River.

Prehistoric man left his imprint on West Virginia in a grand fashion at **Grave Creek Mound,** a massive burial site located just outside of Moundsville. The Adena people, a native Indian tribe, were common to this part of West Virginia and what is now Indiana, Kentucky, Ohio, and Pennsylvania during the Woodland Period, an era lasting from about 1000 B.C. to A.D 700.

The Adena, a hunter-gatherer society, were referred to as the "mound builders" on account of their passion for constructing earthen burial mounds and other earthworks. Grave Creek Mound, now part of the West Virginia State Park System, is the largest and certainly the most impressive of the Adena mounds and is probably the largest conical type of mound ever built. The mound measures 69 feet high; the diameter at the base is 295 feet. The mound was also once encircled by a 40-foot-wide, 5-foot-deep moat. In all about 60,000 tons of earth were moved in the building of the burial place.

Grave Creek Mound, which dates back to 250 B.C., took more than 100 years to build, as evidenced by the multiple burial levels found here. Most of those buried here were probably cremated at death, placed in small log tombs, and covered with earth. Important members of society were often buried in the flesh and laid to rest with valuable personal belongings such as flints, beads, mica, copper ornaments, and pipes.

The story of the Adena and the mounds is told at the adjoining *Delf Norena Museum,* which has an exhaustive collection of artifacts, including an inscribed sandstone tablet (whose meaning is still undetermined) found in the mound during the first excavation in 1838. A gift shop and restaurant also are located in the museum complex. The museum and park are open year-round, except for major holidays, 10:00 A.M. to 4:30 P.M., Monday through Saturday, and 1:00 P.M. to 5:00 P.M., Sunday. There is a nominal admission charge. Call (304) 843–1600 for more information.

If the Adena and their burial grounds seem exotic to you, just wait until you see the next stop on the tour, the *Palace of Gold* in New Vrindaban, a 10-mile trip northeast of Moundsville, in the rolling green hills of Marshall County.

During the late 1960s, when religious and alternate lifestyle communes were cropping up throughout isolated and "live-and-let live" Appalachia, the Hare Krishnas came to this rural stretch of the Northern Panhandle and forever changed the complexion of the place. Between 1973 and 1979, Krishna devotees built this extraordinary palace as a memorial to Srila Prabhupada, founder of the religious movement. Today some 200 residents maintain the sprawling palace—

Burgers with a Twang

*O*kay, what could be less off-the-beaten-path than a McDonald's restaurant? Probably nothing, even if it's in West Virginia. Nevertheless, we believe the McDonald's of Elm Grove legitimately deserves a place in this book. This isn't your run-of-the-mill McDonald's. It's located in Wheeling, at the intersection of the very on-the-beaten paths of National Road and Kruger Street. What's different is everything about this place.

For starters, it's the only McDonald's we know of that boasts live entertainment in a cavernous space-age dining room that can seat more than 500 people! Musical stars from Wheeling's famous Jamboree U.S.A. make regular appearances here, even if it means rolling in a grand piano or staging amplifiers for a full-blown country-and-western band. In addition, the walls and floors here are adorned with spectacular modern art, including museum-quality sculpture.

If the music or the clutter gets to be too much for the little ones, this McDonald's also features a giant soundproof indoor play place—reminiscent of something out of The Jetsons. A kid's paradise for sure. The management will book special receptions, even if it's for an entire busload of folks! Oh, and by the way, the food isn't bad either.

nicknamed "America's Taj Mahal"—and the surrounding 5,000-acre farm. A tour of the 8,000-square-foot palace includes stops in the west gallery, a room laden with marble flooring, giant stained-glass windows, and chandeliers, as well as a peek into the temple room with its awesome mural

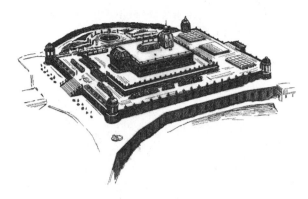

Palace of Gold

containing 4,000 crystals depicting Lord Krishna's life, radiating from the 25-foot-high dome ceiling. Vast gardens and smaller temples are spread out over the compound, which visitors are allowed to roam at will. If you've got visions of Krishnas hounding guests, a la the airports, don't fret: This is a laid-back experience where visitors can tour without intrusions. It's a bit surreal, maybe even excessive, but there's certainly nothing else like it in West Virginia, and for that matter, the nation. If you're a vegetarian, you've come to a Valhalla of sorts. The palace's restaurant is open to the public and it's a gold mine of adventurous veggie dishes with an Indian accent.

The palace and grounds are located off of U.S. 250 in a gorgeous setting of lush hills and pastures. Tours are available daily from April through October, 9:00 A.M. to dark, and from November through March, 10:00 A.M. to 5:00 P.M. The restaurant is open May through October, noon to 4:30 P.M. during weekdays and noon to 8:00 P.M. on weekends. Adult admission to the palace is $5.00; ages six to eighteen, $3.00; and small children are admitted free. For more information, call (304) 843–1812.

There's a tendency among folks who've never been to West Virginia to dismiss **Wheeling** as an industrial has-been, a Rust Belt relic with little or no tourism appeal. Nothing could be further from the truth. Not only is Wheeling loaded with interesting historical and cultural diversions, but it's also a beautiful city with one of the highest concentrations of Victorian homes in the country, lovely parks (including 1,500-acre Oglebay Park, one of the largest and heavily used urban parks in the country), a scenic riverfront, and graceful tree-lined neighborhoods.

This northern city is the birthplace of West Virginia statehood, and you can retrace those tense pre–Civil War times at ***Independence Hall,***

Jamboree in the Hills

Blame it on those "thirtysomething" anxieties— the need to mellow out a bit. Better yet, blame it on the "Jamboree in the Hills," the concert series that plays out each summer in Wheeling. For better or worse, the jamboree helped turned me into a bluegrass music junkie.

Although I've never attended one of the jamborees in person, I had the pleasure of tuning into it live on the radio one fine summer evening while camping at the base of Seneca Rocks. This particular concert featured Ricky Skaggs, Bill Monroe, and Emmylou Harris and the Nash Ramblers. It was a phenomenal show that complemented an incredible evening around the campfire. Hearing Emmylou and the late, great Bill Monroe serve up a rousing version of "Scotland" was by itself enough to convert this one-time country music cynic. Hearing it under the vast West Virginia skies, in the land where so much of this music began, was an experience I'll never forget.

Sixteenth and Market Streets downtown. This stately 1859 Italian Renaissance building was easily the most state-of-the-art structure in Wheeling at the time of the secession debates, claiming both flush toilets and an air-circulating system, a predecessor to modern air-conditioning. The cooling effect was needed for the heated debates that sprung up here in 1861, when it was decided that the western region of Virginia would break free from the rest of the Old Dominion and form its own Union-aligned state, the Reformed State of Virginia. From 1861 to 1863 the Customs House (as it was called then) served as the state capitol. In 1863 President Lincoln declared West Virginia the thirty-fifth state in the Union. Following official statehood the capital moved to Charleston, and the three-story building fell into a number of other uses, including a post office and federal court.

In 1912 Independence Hall was restored, and today it houses exhibits relating to the state's history along with period rooms, an interpretive film, and, from time to time, special historical reenactments. Self-guided tours are free. Group tours with Miss Busbey, an 1860s-attired docent, are $2.00 a person but require a minimum of ten people. Independence Hall is open daily year-round from 10:00 A.M. to 4:00 P.M. except for Sunday in January and February. Call (304) 238–1300.

The Mountain State has always been a hotbed for country music, producing both large audiences and more than its share of performers who've moved on to Nashville. Wheeling is the state's undisputed music capital, thanks to the ongoing success of *Jamboree U.S.A.,* the second-oldest live-radio show in the nation. Every Saturday night since 1933, the country music show has been broadcast over radio station WWVA to fans along the Eastern seaboard and six Canadian provinces. The first show was broadcast on April 1 at midnight at Wheeling's Capitol Theatre; the cost of attending was a whopping 25 cents.

In 1969 the wildly popular show, featuring the rising and established stars of Nashville, moved to its present location at the luxurious *Capitol Music Hall,* 1015 Main Street. Lodged in the middle of downtown, the 2,500-seat theater is heralded for its acoustics and intimate seating. Performers who've graced the stage over the past few years include the likes of Charley Pride, Tom T. Hall, Wynonna Judd, the Statler Brothers, Sammy Kershaw, Crystal Gayle, Roy Clark, Ricky Van Shelton, and the Charlie Daniels Band. Tickets to the shows, almost as coveted as those for West Virginia University football games, are available by calling (800) 624–5456 or dropping by the box office on Main Street. Tickets typically start at about $16 and work their way up depending on the performer.

After the show you can head upstairs to the theater's *Capitol Country Club* for more live country music and dancing, or head over a couple of blocks to the *Cork & Bottle,* 39 Twelfth Street, for a fabulous Greek kabob or steak and probably the best salad bar in the Northern Panhandle. On Friday and Saturday nights, the bar, resembling something out of

Over These Prison Walls

*G*oing to prison in West Virginia might not sound like the best of ideas. But that's exactly what we did one morning in Moundsville, a pretty little community nestled in the hills along the Ohio River just south of Wheeling. We hadn't broken any laws, unless you count a few unnoticed driving infractions. We were in the West Virginia State Penitentiary as part of a tour group, taking in the sites and history of this stark Gothic fieldstone structure, which was built back during the Civil War. Actually, it's no longer a working prison, having shut its doors to felons in 1995.

Today, the abandoned penitentiary is both fascinating and eerie, a reality check of sorts for the public-at-large, which is allowed to tour the facility Tuesday through Sunday from 10 A.M. to 5 P.M. Inside, you'll see where more than ninety men were executed. You'll see the guns used by guards, the isolation tanks where the worst inmates were housed, and yes, even the dreaded electric chair. It's also a great educational experience. We learned, for instance, that West Virginia was indeed the "Wild West" back in the early 1800s, when lawlessness was more or less the norm. We also learned that modern-day West Virginia, while still plagued by the same social problems found everywhere in America, ranks among the lowest of the fifty states in overall crime. That's one bottom ranking West Virginians should be rightly proud of. For tour information, call the West Virginia State Penitentiary at (304) 843-1993, or visit the Web site at http://168.216.221.9/wvhome/n_pan/ marshall/penn.htm.

the French Quarter, stays open until 2 A.M., with live jazz for those who can't get enough music. You can also grab a burger or a Cajun-influenced chicken sandwich, and wash it down with one of the many wines on hand, including some native West Virginia vintages. The Cork & Bottle is open daily 11 A.M. to midnight and on weekends until 2 A.M. Reservations are accepted and encouraged on weekends. Call (304) 232–4400.

Within a few blocks of the Capitol Music Hall, you can stroll the magnificent Victorian homes district. A local group called **Yesterday's Ltd.** (304–233–2003) can arrange for in-house tours and overnight stays. If your idea of nirvana is literally shopping til you drop, then head over to the **Design Company and Gift Shoppe,** 810 Main, where you can browse through an assortment of exquisite handmade arts, crafts, and furniture; stroll through the interior design studio; and then spend the night at the on-site bed-and-breakfast. The stunning eighteen-room town house mansion, operated by proprietors Joe and Gretchen Figaretti, comes with two guest suites, each with a private bath. The shop and studio are open for private tours. Call in advance for tour and/or overnight arrangements at (304) 232–5439.

You really mustn't leave the Wheeling area without a stop at the **Walnut Grove Cemetery,** across the river in Martins Ferry, Ohio. First, this will give you a chance to drive over the **Wheeling Suspension Bridge,** the first bridge over the Ohio River and, at the time of its construction (1849), the longest single-span suspension bridge in the world. With its striking arched stone entrances, the bridge is considered the nation's most important pre–Civil War engineering structure.

Second, a trip to the cemetery, located at the north end of Fourth Street in Martins Ferry, will lead you to the statue and grave of an American hero, Betty Zane. Zane and her family are inextricably linked to Wheeling. The city now stands on the site of Fort Henry, built in 1774 by Colonel Ebenezer Zane and his two brothers, who named the fort for Virginia Governor Patrick Henry. In 1782, what some call the final battle of the Revolutionary War played out here, a battle in which the valiant, young pioneer Betty Zane was a heroine. During that last battle with the Brits, the colonists ran out of ammunition. Colonel Zane's sister volunteered to run through the gunfire to the Zane cabin more than 150 yards away to retrieve more gunpowder for the fort. She was successful, and the Americans withstood the attack. Western and adventure novelist Zane Grey, a descendant of the Zanes, later wrote a novel about Betty and her experiences on the Virginia frontier. The cemetery is open daily from dawn to dusk.

The urban facade of Wheeling gives way to peaceful countryside as you wend your way up State Route 88 to the historic village of Bethany. Here you'll find the redbrick, Roman, Gothic-influenced **Bethany College,** a prestigious liberal arts institution that conjures up images of the film *The Dead Poets Society.* Dominating the ivy- and tree-lined campus, the oldest in West Virginia, is "Old Main," a National Historic Landmark with a 122-foot tower and central building of brick and stone stretching more than 400 feet and punctuated by five arched entrances. It was styled after a similar structure at the University of Glasgow in Scotland.

Also on the college grounds is the **Alexander Campbell Mansion,** the home of Bethany College's founder and a leading figure in the nine-teenth-century religious movement that spawned the Disciples of Christ, Churches of Christ, and Christian Church. The impressive, twenty-five-room home was built in four periods and entertained such important figures of the day as James Garfield, Jefferson Davis, Daniel Webster, and Henry Clay. The mansion is open Tuesday through Sunday, typically from noon to 4:00 P.M., April through October. The rest of the year, tours can be arranged by calling (304) 829–7285.

While on campus you may also want to see the nineteenth-century **Pendleton Heights,** the college president's house, as well as the **Old Bethany Meeting House** and the **Delta Tau Delta Founders' House.**

About a fifteen-minute drive north of Bethany puts you in Weirton, the somewhat gritty but terminally friendly steel-producing town that sits wedged between the Ohio River and the Pennsylvania border. (This part of the Northern Panhandle is barely 5 miles wide.) At first glance Weirton, with its billowing smokestacks and aged brick warehouses, isn't exactly a tourist mecca, but if you look hard enough you'll find that fascinating **industrial tours** are offered by the likes of **Weirton Steel,** one of the town's largest employers and a remarkable business success story. On the tour you'll learn that Weirton Steel, after years of decline, was bought out by its employees in 1984, thus becoming the largest and one of the more profitable employee-owned steel companies in the world. Ernest T. Weir, who founded the company, also founded the city in 1910. Weirton is one of the youngest towns in West Virginia, but it's also one of the most vibrant and lasting company towns. For special tours of Weirton Steel, Starkist Inc., Alpo, Levoler, and other Weirton manufacturers, contact the chamber of commerce at (304) 748–7212, or drop by the office at 3147 West Street.

PLACES TO STAY IN NORTHERN WEST VIRGINIA

KINGWOOD
Heldreth Motel,
State Route 26 South;
(304) 329–1145

TERRA ALTA
Alpine Lake Resort,
State Route 7;
(304) 789–2481

FAIRMONT
Holiday Inn,
I–79 and Grafton Road;
(304) 366–5500

Days Inn,
I–79, exit 133;
(304) 367–1370

MORGANTOWN
EconoLodge Coliseum,
I–79, exit 155;
(304) 599–8181

Holiday Inn,
1400 Saratoga Avenue;
(304) 599–1680

WHEELING
Comfort Inn,
I–70, exit 11;
(304) 547–1880

The Eckhart house,
810 Main Street;
(304) 232–5439

Mclure House Hotel and
Convention Center,
1200 Market Street;
(800) 862–5873

Hampton Inn,
I–70, exit 2A;
(304) 233–0440

PLACES TO EAT IN NORTHERN WEST VIRGINIA (ALL AREA CODES 304)

KINGWOOD
Heldreth Restaurant and
Lounge,
State Route 26 South;
329–1147

TERRA ALTA
Alpine Lake Resort,
State Route 7;
789–2481

FAIRMONT
Holiday Inn,
I–79 and Old Grafton
Road; 366–5500

MORGANTOWN
The Restaurants of Historic
Downtown Morgantown
(40 restaurants within 1-
mile radius), I–68, exit 1
University Avenue;
292–0168

WHEELING
McDonald's of Elm Grove,
National Road and
Kruger Street; 242–3693

Oglebay Resort,
State Route 88 North;
243–4000

Undo's Italian Restaurant
(McLure House Hotel),
1200 Market Street;
232–0300

Abbey's,
145 Zane Street;
232–0729

The Anchor Room
669 Main Street;
527–0080

Nail City Brewing Company
(Artisan Center at Heritage
Square),
1400 Main Street;
233–5330

FOR MORE INFORMATION

Greater Morgantown
Convention and Visitors
Bureau; (304) 292–5081

Wheeling Convention and
Visitors Bureau;
(304) 233–7709

Index

INDEX

INDEX

INDEX

INDEX

INDEX

About the Authors

Stephen Soltis is a freelance writer and part-time resident of West Virginia, where he owns a cabin on the eastern slope of Short Mountain. He is the author of *The Insiders' Guide to Metropolitan Washington, D.C.,* (published by the *Richmond Times-Dispatch*) and was a business and regional travel writer for four years at the *Washington Flyer,* the nation's first in-airport magazine, for which he also wrote numerous articles on travel in West Virginia. Prior to moving to his current residence in Atlanta, Georgia, where he is employed as an executive speechwriter, he lived in Washington, D.C., for seven years, during which time he traveled tens of thousands of miles throughout West Virginia in search of its hidden nooks and crannies.

Stacy Soltis has spent the past eleven years writing for business publications and in corporate communications in and around the Washington, D.C., area. A native of Arkansas, she has spent the better part of her married life combing the hills and valleys of West Virginia with husband Steve, a fellow Mountain State devotee. She now lives in Atlanta with her husband and children and is pursuing a career in collegiate public relations.

Devoted to Travelers
Diverse in Nature